Margaret Howard's Pick of the Week

Published by arrangement with
the British Broadcasting Corporation

Margaret Howard's
PICK OF THE WEEK

Illustrated by Merrily Harpur

Hutchinson
London Melbourne Sydney Auckland Johannesburg

Hutchinson and Co. (Publishers) Ltd
An imprint of the Hutchinson Publishing Group
17–21 Conway Street, London W1P 6JD

Hutchinson Publishing Group (Australia) Pty Ltd
16–22 Church Street, Hawthorn, Melbourne, Victoria 3122

Hutchinson Group (NZ) Ltd
32–34 View Road, PO Box 40-086, Glenfield, Auckland 10

Hutchinson Group (SA) Pty Ltd
PO Box 337, Bergvlei 2012, South Africa

First published 1984

Set in Linotron Sabon and Helvetica Light by
Tradespools Ltd, Frome, Somerset

Printed and bound in Great Britain by
Butler & Tanner Ltd, Frome and London

British Library Cataloguing in Publication Data

Margaret Howard's Pick of the week.
1. Anecdotes
I. Howard, Margaret
828'.91402'08   PN6261
ISBN 0 09 158810 3

For Moomin
who never heard Pick of the Week
but would have loved it

Introduction

Pick of the Week is twenty-five years old this year. The series began in April 1959 – the same year, curiously enough, as my first broadcast. This event went unmarked, I may say, and hardly surprisingly since it was rather unexpected and unplanned. I was a very young apprentice BBC studio manager at the time, assigned to do the sound effects on *Listen with Mother*. On this particular occasion, there was a story about some pigs, I seem to remember, and I was required to ring a bicycle bell on cue, although what the pigs were doing on bicycles I can't quite recall. Now, if you have ever tried to get a bicycle bell to ring exactly when you want it to, you will have some idea of my difficulty. Suffice it to say that, after several rehearsals where all I managed to produce were a few strangulated clunks and clinks, the exasperated producer said to me, 'For God's sake, dear, say ting-a-ling.' And so my career at the microphone began.

In 1974 I was asked to do *Pick of the Week*. The programme had been started by Gale Pedrick, based on an idea by Claire Lowson-Dick, who made his selection from the week's broadcasts and then wrote a script which was read by somebody else. John Ellison was the name associated with the programme in the early days and indeed he continued to present it when Nancy Wise joined the team. By the time I came along, the BBC was in search of a new voice to introduce the programme, as John Ellison had retired because of ill health. Helen Fry, the chief producer in the department that makes the programme, then asked me to do *Pick of the Week* and the revolutionary idea was that I should both select and present the hour-long programme on the air. It's hard to remember it now but there were not nearly so many women on the air in those days. The news was read by men;

7

reporters and correspondents were mostly men. Apart from the statutory woman to introduce *Woman's Hour*, female voices were scarce. It was felt that listeners might react unfavourably. However, after due consideration, it was decided that I should be given a chance, on the understanding that if it didn't work I should return to the back room, never to be heard in voice again. I am happy to say that I have been behind the microphone ever since.

This book is a selection of some of my favourite broadcasts. They have all featured on the programme at some time during the last few years; the earliest dates from 1979. People often ask me how I manage to do *Pick of the Week*. They seem to imagine that producers and contributors are beating a path to my door, pressing extracts upon me, or that I have a vast team of listeners who inundate me with ideas. However, the 'team' consists of only two people – a producer, a different one each week out of a rota of six, and a researcher. The researcher is responsible for physically assembling all the tape recordings I need every week, and for finding a way through what I call the contractual minefield. As soon as I choose something, the researcher must find out if we have the right to re-broadcast it and, if so, on what terms. Sometimes an idea will have to be dropped because it is simply too expensive or because the original contract permits no repeats. Certain union agreements governing length of extracts have to be observed. If I select an item featuring a member of the royal family, a transcript has to be sent to the palace and royal assent for re-broadcasting sought. It is not always granted.

The other member of the team, the producer, sits with me in my office at Broadcasting House. We compare notes on what we may have heard beforehand and then plough our way through the tape recordings we have managed to get in advance of programmes being broadcast, at the same time keeping an ear open for live events. Sometimes we have three programmes going at once; certainly that is often the case in my house: I have a radio set in every corner and a television upstairs and down, plus a video recorder. When I am not listening to them, I leap into the car and listen to the radio as I sit in traffic jams. If it all sounds a bit like bedlam, well, it is, at times. Of course, by no means do I manage to hear everything. I did consider wearing headphones on horseback but decided it would be too dangerous! My Jack Russell looks exactly like the HMV dog, so he is clearly geared for

8

listening and is quite good at not interrupting.

Then there are the moments when, through all the din, I suddenly hear that gem; I pause in recognition of the indefinable quality that makes a broadcast a candidate for *Pick of the Week*.

Margaret Howard
June 1984

Author's Note

I am grateful to Helen Fry, chief producer in Archive Features Radio, whose idea it was to ask me to do *Pick of the Week* in the first place and who has been a constant source of help and support to me ever since.

I am also indebted to my immediate predecessor, Nancy Wise, from whom I inherited a well-organized, smooth-running operation, and to Gale Pedrick who started it all.

My thanks to all those BBC editors, producers, reporters, writers and contributors of all kinds who each week provide me with the material I need to make up my programme. Particular thanks to those who send me copies of their scripts well in advance!

My 'team' consists each week of one producer, drawn from the Archive Features Unit, to whom I am ever grateful. I am sure none of them will mind if I single out Phyllis Robinson who was with the programme right from the start. We also have a secretary and, the linchpin of the whole thing, the research assistant. I have been fortunate in having wonderfully hard-working and loyal researchers during time on *Pick of the Week*. Jill Meyer and Barbara Phillips have long since left to have babies. Ailsa Hornsby now researches for MPs in the House of Commons and Lucy Geidt, my most recent helper, ever to be remembered for her great tenacity, is even now terriering away on a Radio 4 current affairs programme. I am deeply grateful to them for all their help and good humoured devotion to me and the programme. Cairney Down now takes on the mantle of the *Pick of the Week* researcher and it is she who undertook the enormous task of helping me to find all the pieces for this book. May her patience be rewarded!

Since this is my first time in print, I would like to thank my publishers for their encouragement, particularly Roger Houghton who thought of the book and Joanna Edwards who helped me prepare it for the printer.

One thing I am always on the lookout for when making my selection for *Pick of the Week* is a good noise: the plaintive cry of a whale, the deep, deep sound of Tibetan monks chanting, or the mating call of the haddock. Perhaps you remember hearing that delicious crisp crunch of the close-up recording of a Roman snail biting into a Webb's Wonder lettuce, or the delightful snufflings in the long grass as a hedgehog whirled round and round in his courtship dance?

Then there was the man who played Mozart's *Rondo à la Turque* by tapping an HB pencil on his teeth. That was followed by a whole spate of people making music with their bodies. Some hit themselves with spanners to get a tune, others deliberately tapped their Adam's apples

with a finger to give a new resonance to the *William Tell Overture* or 'God Save the Queen'.

It is difficult to give you a feeling of such noises in print, but not impossible, thanks to the poet Edwin Morgan. On a School Radio programme called *Word Games* I heard his poem 'The Loch Ness Monster's Song'. There are no recognizable words in it. It is simply a sequence of sounds. I recommend that you read it aloud, and if you pronounce every letter and every syllable you should end up doing a fairly creditable imitation of Nessie!

> Sssnnnwhufffll?
> Hnwhuffl hhnnwfl hnfl hfl?
> Gdroblboblhobngbl gbl gl gg g g g glbgl.
> Drublhaflablhaflubhafgabhaflhafl fl fl –
> bm grawwww grf grawf awfgm graw gm.
> Hovoplodok-doplodovok-plovodokot-doplodokosh?
> Splgraw fok fok splgrafhatchgabrlgabrl fok splfok!
> Zgra kra gka fok!
> Grof grawff gahf?
>
> Gombl mbl bl-
> blm plm,
> blm plm,
> blm plm,
> blp.

●

A similar delight in sounds for the sake of what they can evoke was evident on Radio 4's light-entertainment programme *Whizzalongawavelength*. The *Whizzalong* team called themselves the National Revue Company. Like all broadcasters, they had itchy feet and yearned to do what is known in the business as an OB, an outside broadcast. In a special European edition they joined up with radio stations on the continent – or so they said. What follows is a snappy contribution from Radio Aix-en-Provence, invented by Geoffrey Perkins, who brought a terrific amount of dash and élan to the reading of it.

Vous vous régalez des délices aériens hyper-hyper chouettes de radio Aix-en-Provence qui vous transporte sur les ondes (mille deux cent mètres) avec la musique super-boum; eh ouais ça gaze là ça gaze, et dansez clunque à la funque 'Strut Your Rump to the Funk'; bon bon aujourd'hui je vous offre une bonne selection de big hits – vous allez voir ce que je veux dire, d'abord the Police et 'De Doo Doo Doo, De Dah Dah Dah', puis les Crystals avec 'Da Doo Ron Ron', en plus pas mal d'autres chansons célèbres, par exemple 'Be Bop A Lula', 'Boom Bang A Bang', 'Ding-A-Ling', 'Dick-A-Dum-Dum', 'Doo-wah Diddy Diddy Dum Diddy Day', 'Papa Oom Mow Mow', 'Wakka Doo Wakka Day', 'Doobeedood'n'Doobe Doobeedood'n'Doobe', 'Loo-be-loo', 'Loop Di Love', 'La La La', 'La Di Dah', 'Ga Ga Ga'.

●

Naivety about words and ignorance of double meanings led to one of the most famous broadcasting boobs. It was in a School Radio programme some years back. The events were recalled by John Dunn in a sixtieth-anniversary tribute to School Radio entitled *Faith, Hope and Clarity* – the motto they had adopted for themselves when they started broadcasts for the classroom on 24 April 1924. John Dunn reminded everyone of the story and added a little anecdote of his own at the end.

John Dunn: It happened in a music and movement programme. Joan Paterson was one of the studio managers in the control room and she was listening to a rehearsal of the programme.

Joan Paterson: Perhaps my mind had just drifted in another direction for a second and I suddenly heard my colleague saying, 'She can't say that!' And I said, 'Say what?' 'Well,' he said, 'you listen.' And I started to listen very hard. And I said, 'What are we going to do?' because she was having a lovely little game for children where she said, 'This is a ball game. Now you throw your balls up in the air ...' Now you do this and you do that ... now you play with your balls, and so on and so forth. And my colleague said, 'It's no good. You'll have to tell her.' I said, 'I can't tell her. You go and tell her.' He went into the studio and he said, 'You know, I don't think you can say some of those things.' She said, 'Say what things?' 'Well this exercise about the balls, you see.' 'What's wrong with it? A ball is a ball.'

Archive recording: And now the music is going to tell you where your balls are. They may be high up so that you have to stretch and jump up for them. Or they may be low down so that you have to pick them up off the floor. Listen – *(high-pitched piano playing)* – well, were your balls high up or low down? They were

13

high up and I hope you've all jumped up and got them. Now dance round and toss them in the air and play with them.

John Dunn: As a matter of fact I recall a similar incident in a Schools programme. It was a dramatization of an old Polish rural folk tale, I think, about a farming family and a little boy who looked after all the chickens. And we all had the greatest difficulty in persuading the lady producer that she perhaps shouldn't let this young lad go round saying, 'But, granny, I've got the biggest – male hen – in the village!'

•

Despite little semantic difficulties such as these, you would think that we have enough languages on this earth to be able to communicate with one another without the need to invent a new one. However, not just one but 500 or so attempts have been made to establish an international language. So far, each attempt has singularly failed, judging from the delightfully dotty spokesmen Richard Stilgoe found for his series *Potted Tongues*. Many of them were the sole custodians and only speakers of the tongue of their own devising. Esperanto is the one artificial language we have all heard of, and it is perhaps the most successful – but even that is a long way from being a *lingua franca*.

Richard Stilgoe: If Esperanto survives, and actually works, it's after a good few sliced linguistic drives. Daddy of them all was Descartes, who in 1629 sketched out the rules for a language. But the first real donkey work was done by Sir Thomas Urquhart in 1653, who invented Logopandekteision in his home in Cromarty: *Logopandekteision, or an Introduction to the Universal Language, Digested into Six Several Books by Sir Thomas Urquhart, of Cromarty, Knight.*

Will Green: Each had an enormous name, one of them was Chryseomystes. Another was Neleodicastes. It was a non-starter, didn't get very far.

Richard Stilgoe: So not only in Cromarty, but also in Forth, Biscay, Tyne, Dover, Portland, Dogger and Heligoland – language collector Will Green reports that they were all at it.

Will Green: None of them achieved any success and most of them were simple projects. French and English have been combined in

14

an attempt to produce a world language on more than one occasion. German and French, Spanish with English, Spanish with French. Reformation of Latin will be Novi Latine, or Latino Sine Flexione – that's Latin without inflection, as you might have guessed. Latinesco, Mondilatin ... then there was Latino Macaronico produced in Italy. And then were many scatter-brained ideas besides – for instance, a language based on the seven colours of the rainbow. Also, which was not unrelated, someone wanted to produce language based on seven musical notes.

Richard Stilgoe: Solresol, the Universal Language, by François Sudre. Here at last a really impartial language, acceptable to all men, easy to speak, to read, to write, to pronounce, and to spell. Solresol will become a second language for all the inhabitants of the earth.

Will Green: The idea being that music is already international, isn't it? So if you can make millions of tunes which are distinguishable, surely you can make millions, or thousands, of words. So he created a language, or tried to create a language, based on the notes which you could sing.

Richard Stilgoe: Solresol is a lovely idea. Jean François Sudre decided in 1817 that, since every child learned the tonic solfa – he knew they did because he was a teacher – he would use only the syllables *doh re me fa soh la ti* and make all his words out of those. So, after purchasing his dictionary from the Library of Progress, together with a *Solresol Grammar* by Professor Gojewski, I should be able to say things like: 'Solmisolmi, solladofa re sollamifa mifadomi fasi solrefasol soldoredo.' Got it?

●

To follow all those strange new words, let's have a definition of a very familiar one. I heard it one week in December on Radio 4's *Bookshelf*, at a time when one is almost overwhelmed by preparations for the festive season. Last posting dates were whizzing by, the turkey had not been ordered, and I was already being asked to appear on a programme about New Year's resolutions, when I heard this quote from *The Enlarged Devil's Dictionary* by Ambrose Bierce:

Christmas: Noun. A day set apart and consecrated to gluttony, drunkenness, maudlin sentiment, gift taking, public dullness and domestic behaviour.

In my view, it has never been better expressed.

The most fascinating part of any dictionary, I think, is the bit that tells you the derivation of a word. Often when looking something up, perhaps purely to see how it is spelled, I get lost meandering through the pages to other words which oddly and delightfully have sprung from Old French or Early Norse or just plain old Anglo-Saxon. That is one of the reasons I enjoy appearing on *Call My Bluff* so much – although quite often on that programme the invented definitions are more fun than the real ones.

The real meanings behind the names of some of our flowers were explained by Denis Owen in one of his talks in the series *What's in a Name?* He also gave a guide to their proper pronunciation. For instance, the 'pint' in cuckoo pint is pronounced not as in 'pint of milk' but as in 'pin-table'.

Some of his definitions were distinctly saucy – though the origin of the pansy seemed straightforward enough.

The word 'pansy' is believed to be derived from the French *penser*, to think. The name comes from the way the flower hangs its head, as if in thought, half hiding its face. One English common name is paunce, spelt p-a-u-n-c-e, which seems a direct rendering of the French

Pansies certainly do hang their heads in a demure sort of way, but I think it is the hiding of the face, and looking down shyly, like Princess Di, that is responsible for many of the older names, some of them oddly amorous. There's:

> Three faces under a hood (a reference to the three flower colours)
> Love in idleness
> Cuddle me to you
> Jump up and kiss me
> Kiss me at the garden gate
> Tittle my fancy

and Heartsease, which is said to indicate a medicinal value – it is good for passions of the heart.

Another plant with lots of names is the wild arum, the common wild lily of our hedgerows, with its long, spike-like flowers, spotted leaves and red fruit. It's often called lords and ladies, or cuckoo pint.

The word 'pint' (not peint) is from the Old English and Old

16

German *pintle*, meaning penis, and refers to the long flower spike. 'Cuckoo' means that it appears when the cuckoos first arrive in spring. It has also been called, in different parts of the country, wake-pintle and priest's pintle.

And I think it's the plant in Shakespeare's *Hamlet*, Act IV, Scene 7:

> 'Of crow-flowers, daisies, and long purples
> That liberal shepherds give a grosser name
> But our cold maids do dead men's fingers call them.'

Some think that Shakespeare's long purples are the early purple orchid, which also has spotted leaves. The orchid also has root tubers, which are supposed to resemble dead men's fingers. But I'll bet it's the cuckoo pint.

Lords and ladies is a more recent name – introduced, I think, in an attempt to 'clean up' the English common names for plants and animals, some of which were positively vulgar, though at the same time aptly descriptive. The white or purple flower spikes have a fanciful resemblance to the colourful dress of lords and ladies. Perhaps another common name, parson in the pulpit, is considered a more polite replacement for priest's pintle.

●

As far as I know, a priest's pintle has not been preserved as a religious relic, but various other remains of holy persons have been treasured as objects of devotion. For a Radio 4 programme called *Holy Bones*, Libby Purves looked into the whole business of religious relics and came across some pretty strange antiquities in the process. In one collection alone she saw a bone of St Aloysius, part of the jaw of the Blessed Ambrose Barlow, a fragment of St Thomas More's hair, dried blood, ancient linen and parts of teeth.

To religious people there is nothing so very strange about all this. Others feel that keeping relics is a medieval practice that should be abandoned. It was certainly in the Middle Ages, as Libby Purves pointed out, that the cult of religious relics flourished.

Libby Purves: Monasteries and churches would claim ownership of a drop of Mary's milk, or the tip of Lucifer's tail, St Joseph's breath in a bottle, the rod of Moses, or the tears of Christ. There were tales of people blasted to death when they approached relics impiously – or of house fires driven back, miraculously, by a relic of Thomas à Becket tied to a long pole; and objects were said to double their weight and to glow by a sort of divine radioactivity after being placed near a relic.

The earthly practicalities of the medieval world also led to practices which make modern observers flinch. Thomas Aquinas's body was dismembered and the flesh boiled from the bone; it was only in the year 1299 that Pope Boniface VIII banned the boiling of holy people's bodies inside churches. Such zealous excesses were not the work of fanatics, but often of devout, mainstream men of the church. The most dramatic tale is of the saintly Bishop, Hugh of Lincoln.

He was a learned monk, a great builder of schools – and a liberal who risked his life to save Jews from death in a riot. He was devout and holy. He was also a man of his time when it came to relic-seeking.

Reader: When he was at the celebrated monastery of Fécamp, he extracted, by biting, two small fragments of the bone of the arm of the most blessed lover of Christ, Mary Magdalen ...

This bone had never been seen divested of its wrappings by the

abbot or any of the monks who were present on that occasion, for it was sewn very tightly into three cloths – two of silk and one of ordinary linen.

They did not dare to accede even to the bishop's prayer to be allowed to see it. He, however, taking a small knife from one of his notaries, hurriedly cut the thread and undid the wrappings. After reverently examining and kissing the much venerated bone, he tried unsuccessfully to break it with his fingers, and then bit it, first with his incisors and, finally, with his molars. By this means he broke off the two fragments which he handed immediately to me, with the words: 'Take charge of this for me with especial care.'

When the abbot and monks saw what had happened, they were first overcome with horror, and then became exceedingly enraged. They cried out, 'What terrible profanity! We thought that the bishop had asked to see this holy and venerable relic for reasons of devotion, and he has stuck his teeth into it and gnawed it as if he were a dog.' He mollified their anger with soothing words: 'If, a little while ago, I handled the most sacred body of the Lord of all the saints with my fingers, in spite of my unworthiness, and when I partook of it, touched it with my lips and teeth, why should I not venture to treat in the same way the bones of the saints for my protection, and by this commemoration of them increase my reverence for them, and without profanity acquire them when I have the opportunity?'

●

Edmund Gosse, who later became well known as a translator, critic and literary historian, started his working life as a clerk in the Reading Room of the British Museum. He came to London from his home in Torquay at the age of seventeen in the year 1867, leaving behind his anxious parents.

We have heard a lot of late about Victorian virtues, and certainly Gosse senior seemed to enshrine them. He was determined that, though his son was far away, he should not lack the benefit of fatherly advice on matters both temporal and spiritual. The result was that poor Edmund's breakfast at his Tottenham lodgings was regularly and thoroughly spoiled by the arrival of an almost daily paternal missive. 'There it would lie awaiting me,' he said, 'destroying the taste of the bacon, reducing the flavour of the tea to insipidity.'

Edmund Gosse's biographer, Ann Thwaite, collected some of these letters together for a series of programmes on Radio 3 called *Father to Son*. The one that follows is dated 30 January 1867.

On Saturday morning we had the long-desired tidings of your having actually commenced work. While there are disappointments associated with it, as the earlier hour of attendance, and no Saturday holiday, on the other hand we notice with thankfulness that you have been assigned to the pleasanter of the two rooms, and have agreeable companions. Remember my counsel of being chary of yielding your intimacy, until you know that the persons seeking it are safe and worthy. And don't be afraid of letting it be known that *you* are Christ's. Show your colours.

There is yet much of your occupation of which we look to learn more, but can wait till you find convenient time. We know that it is not now the same as it was a week ago with you.

Therefore, however much we long to hear of your matters in detail, we will curb our impatience and make allowance for you. But try to keep up the Journal if possible; even if you are able to add only a few lines every evening. I do not expect you will continue to feel the fatigue so sensibly as at first; you will soon get into training, and will, after a few weeks, hardly feel the walking. And the spring mornings will soon make the early rising bearable.

The amount you paid for carriage of your goods, and the carpenter's help, and the frames was all very reasonable. When you tell me that 'of the £5 note 2-stroke-3 remain', I am at a loss whether to read the '2-stroke-3' as 'two thirds' of the £5, or as 'two shillings and threepence'; for the figures may mean either. If the former, your expenditure has been quite economical; if the latter, I can give no opinion till you give me the particulars how it has been spent. I certainly did not imagine that Five Pounds would be exhausted in three weeks, without board. The former is, however, far the more likely; but please tell me distinctly. You are keeping, of course, an exact account of it.

I am glad Mr Naage was pleased with your writing: may your spelling pass muster as well. Probably it is owing to your having been so very tired when writing that there are more than usual slips. I think I will regularly return you the mis-spelled words on a separate bit of paper; and I recommend that you should carefully correct them, *in writing* (not merely in your mind); you need not send the paper back to me, but carefully preserve them, and occasionally refer to them.

I cannot imagine how your Museum office can be 'near the gates'. What gates?

Mamma was exceedingly pleased with your nice plan of your

room, so clear and neat and intelligible; and she is very much obliged, and is glad it is so pleasant. The altered direction of the bed is a great improvement. May you often be very happy there; when none but God is your companion, and the holy angels your witnesses. Now once more, adieu! Every grace and blessing upon you I beseech, with fervent and incessant prayers, from our loving Lord.

Ever, my dear Son,
Your tender Father,
P. H. Gosse

•

Just occasionally, something I choose for *Pick of the Week* sparks off an instant reaction. The letters come flooding in asking for a transcript of whatever it might be. It is usually a poem that strikes some sort of national chord. Such was the case when I re-played part of Radio 4's *Morning Service*.

It was from St George's Church, Taunton, and the sermon was preached by the Reverend Father David Kiely. His theme was the importance of listening, and to illustrate it he read out a poem. The poem had been written by an old lady and had been found in a hospital locker after her death. It was addressed to the nurses and clearly reflected the way she had felt in the last months of her life. To those around her she seemed like a senile old fool but underneath she knew the girl and the young woman she had been.

Look Closer

What do you see nurses, what do you see?
Are you thinking when you're looking at me
A crabbed old woman not very wise.
Uncertain of habit with far-away eyes.
Who dribbles her food and makes no reply,
When you say in a loud voice, I do wish you'd try.
I'll tell you who I am, as I sit here so still,
As I rise to your bidding, as I eat at your will.
I'm a small child of ten, with a father and mother,
Brothers and sisters who love one another.
A bride soon at twenty. My heart gives a leap
Remembering the vows that I promised to keep.
At twenty-five now I have young of my own

Who need me to build a secure happy home.
At fifty once more children play round my knee,
Again we know children, my beloved and me.

Dark days are upon me. My husband is dead.
I look to the future, I shudder with dread.
My young are too busy rearing young of their own,
And I think of the years and the love I have known.
I'm an old woman now and nature is cruel.
'Tis her jest to make old age look like a fool.
The body it crumbles, grace and vigour depart.
There is now a stone where I once had a heart.
But inside this old carcass a young girl still dwells,
And I'm loving and living all over again;
And I think of the years all too few gone, too fast,
And accept a stark fact that nothing will last.
So open your eyes nurse, open and see,
Not a crabbed old woman, look closer, see me.

●

A few weeks later, I had a call from the BBC in Glasgow to say that,
following my broadcast of the poem, they had used it on one of their own
local programmes, *Macgregor's Gathering*, hosted by the folk singer
Jimmie Macgregor. That broadcast prompted a listener to send in another
poem written by Liz Hogben (SRN) in answer to the first. It was called 'A
Nurse's Reply'.

What do we see, you ask, what do we see?
Yes, we are thinking when looking at thee!
We may seem to be hard when we hurry and fuss,
But there's many of you, and too few of us.
We would like far more time to sit by you and talk,
To bath you and feed you and help you to walk.
To hear of your lives and the things you have done:
Your childhood, your husband, your daughter, your son.
But time is against us, there's too much to do —
Patients too many, and nurses too few.
We grieve when we see you so sad and alone,
With nobody near you, no friends of your own.
We feel all your pain, and know of your fear
That nobody cares now your end is so near.

But nurses are people with feelings as well,
And when we're together you'll often hear tell
Of the dearest old Gran in the very end bed,
And the lovely old Dad, and the things that he said.
We speak with compassion and love, and feel sad
When we think of your lives and the joy that you've had.
When the time has arrived for you to depart,
You leave us behind with an ache in our heart.

When you sleep the long sleep, no more worry or care,
There are other old people, and we must be there.
So please understand if we hurry and fuss –
There are many of you, and too few of us.

●

Nursing is one of the professions traditionally open to women. Until quite
recently, for a woman to want to aspire to higher callings – to be a doctor,
say – was regarded as decidedly uppity. Obstacles were put in her way. In
my own case, when I was a BBC announcer and suggested that perhaps I
might be allowed to read the news, I was firmly told that that was man's
work. Nobody would believe the news if it was read by a woman, they said.
Happily that has all changed now. Women can be doctors and
newsreaders and a lot else besides. But it was not achieved without a
struggle and by no means all the battles have been won yet.
   It suits society economically to keep women in a secondary role, a role
where they need not necessarily get paid at all, and yet form an important
part of the labour force. It's a situation that was clearly described by the
American economist J. K. Galbraith, whose book *Economics and the
Public Purpose* was quoted in a BBC World Service series called *Women
of the World*.

The conversion of women into a crypto-servant class was an
economic accomplishment of the first importance. Menially
employed servants were available only to a minority of the pre-
industrial population; the servant–wife is available, democrati-
cally, to almost the entire present male population. Were the
workers so employed subject to pecuniary compensation, they
would be by far the largest single category in the labour force.

●

23

Women of the World was a major World Service series in which Natalie Wheen and Jenyth Worsley examined the position of women in society today across many cultures and nationalities.

In our own country there are many women who have managed to succeed in what has hitherto been a man's world – notably, the Prime Minister, the Rt. Hon. Mrs Margaret Thatcher. She agreed to be interviewed for the programme and, amongst other things, she gave her view of why it is that women find it difficult to get to the top.

There aren't any women editors of national newspapers. Why? There are a lot of women journalists; there have been women financial journalists. We haven't had a woman Director of the BBC yet; though we have had many very powerful women in radio and in television.

I always get very cross when women say, 'I'm just a housewife.' Running a home is a managerial job, and therefore some of them do not wish to take on the added responsibility of climbing their own tree. And so when it comes to the last step to the top, you haven't got enough to choose from; there's all the intermediate layers on the way up, and that's really where we've got to get the extra ambition going. So you have got these problems, you can't duck them; but there are many, many women who have the opportunities and who do not use them, or who are too easily contented with the job that they are doing and who do not necessarily make the effort to climb the tree. Sometimes it's thought to be unfeminine to do that – it isn't at all, you know.

The most crucial moment for Mrs Thatcher when climbing to the top of her particular tree was in 1974, when she stood for election as leader of the Conservative Party against Edward Heath.

Margaret Thatcher: That was really, I suppose, the greatest opportunity of all which came along, and I knew the prejudices against women in the top job. But I think we look too much at 'women' and 'men' in jobs; I think if we looked much more at the appropriate personality, we shouldn't be surprised that sometimes women get on.

Natalie Wheen: You talked about prejudices against women in power, and there was prejudice certainly when you got to the top. Did none of that weigh up against you? Was it difficult?

Margaret Thatcher: I don't know. I think it weighs against you until you become known, not as a woman politician, but as a personality. You see, really to me the whole secret of life is to stop looking at things in terms of men politicians, women politicians, men in power, women in power. You come to a certain time when you look at the personalities available and their policies and you forget whether they're men or women. And really that's how women have got on, because they've had the right personality with the right capability in the right place at the right time. And there have been people who were prepared to look at them as personalities. I always think that one of the great reasons for the advance of legislation in favour of women – 1882, for example, only just over a century ago, the Married Women's Property Act: until then married women weren't allowed to have any property, it belonged to their husband – I think a lot of this came, as women became more and more educated, from men who saw their educated daughters, and who saw their daughters of considerable talent and ability, and who just weren't prepared to look at them as second-class citizens, and so gradually they brought in the legislation. It's astonishing that it took so long, but then I suppose in the past women have exerted influence in different ways.

Natalie Wheen: We've talked about male aggression, but there's another kind of aggression, isn't there?

Jenyth Worsley: Well, there's certainly female aggression. Do you find that women are particularly acid, as it were, because they would like to be in your place?

Margaret Thatcher: I don't find women acid. I don't think any woman in power or any woman in life will really have a happy life unless she's got a large number of women friends. Don't you find the same thing? You really must ... You both understand that frequently it's women who are left to cope. You can't hand over your responsibilities for a family to anyone else. You find it throughout life. You find it in wartime; women did remarkable things in wartime. Why were men so astonished? I don't know. Why were people so astonished? Why sometimes were they so damnably patronizing about it? No, I don't find women acid. One values those friendships enormously. Indeed, sometimes you wouldn't be able to carry on without them, because you sometimes must go and sit down and let down your hair with someone you can trust totally, who understands similar things and who'll just talk. I mean, I find it very easy to talk to Mrs Gandhi because I suppose that she and I are two women who have something in common that no one else has; and we understand the combination of that pull of family and the total dedication to politics and how you simply cannot get on in politics unless your family are behind you. I mean, Denis has been absolutely marvellous – in my earliest days when I was married, recognizing that one has these talents and abilities and it would be an awful mistake not to use them – so one had the most marvellous encouragement. What else do you need if you have family and friends? You can get through anything; much more important than riches.

•

More than family, friends and power, the seventeenth-century Duchess of Newcastle, Margaret Cavendish, wanted to be remembered. 'I fear my ambition inclines towards vainglory,' she wrote, '... which is to live by

26

remembrance in after ages.' This is an ambition that has been fulfilled; her writings were recalled on Radio 3 in a programme compiled by Kathleen Jones.

When Margaret Cavendish first started to publish books, it was generally thought that they must have been written by someone else and printed in her name. They thought it, she said, 'impossible that a woman could have so much learning and understanding in terms of art and scholastical expressions.' Such was the doubt about her capacity that her husband was moved to write an epistle in her vindication in the front of one of her works, confirming that what was written and printed in her name was indeed her own.

Perhaps, in the light of all that, it is not surprising to discover that Margaret Cavendish was an early feminist.

It is not only uncivil and ignoble, but unnatural for men to speak against women and their liberties. True it is that men from their first creation usurped a supremacy to themselves, although we were made equal by nature, which tyrannical government they have kept ever since, so that we never come to be free, but rather more and more enslaved, using us either like children, fools or subjects – which slavery has so dejected our spirits as we are become so stupid that beasts are but a degree below us; whereas in nature we have as clear an understanding as men, if we were bred in schools to mature our brains and manure our understandings that we might bring forth the fruits of knowledge.

Alas, men that are not only our tyrants but our devils keep us in the hell of subjection, from whence I cannot perceive any redemption or getting out. We may complain, and bewail our condition, yet that will not free us – our words to men are as empty sounds, our sighs as puffs of wind, our tears as fruitless showers, and our power is so inconsiderable as men laugh at our weaknesses.

So we are become like worms that live in the dull earth of ignorance, winding ourselves sometimes out by the help of some refreshing rain of good education, which seldom is given us, for we are kept like birds in cages, to hop up and down in our houses, not suffered to fly abroad. Thus, by an opinion in men, we are shut out of all power and authority, our counsels are despised and laughed at, the best of our actions are trodden down with scorn, by the over-weening conceit men have of themselves and through a despisement of us.

It is to be hoped, 300 years later, that men are more understanding and enlightened. Mel Smith and Griff Rhys Jones in head-to-head conversation on BBC2's *Alas Smith and Jones* presented, perhaps, a typical picture of the male view of feminism today.

Mel: What, er, what are your thoughts on the women's movement then? Actually?

Griff: Well . . . eh?

Mel: What do you think about the women's movement?

Griff: Well, it's all right, y'know. She's up and down a bit but she doesn't move about much. When we was first married . . . she use to wiggle about . . .

Mel: No, no. See what that is? What that is is a sexist remark. You are being sexist.

Griff: I'm not being sexist. I'm not. I've had a talk with my wife, right, and we've agreed that she's an individual, right, and I say she can do what she likes . . . As long as my tea's on the table, I don't give a monkey's. She can go out and go down the launderette and do the ironing and all that . . . whenever she wants to. She can do her cleaning job and she's free . . . she's a free lady.

Mel (pausing): You know my wife's sister. She went . . . er, she went down to Greenham Common last weekend. Yeah, she's, er, been down there quite a lot.

Griff: Oh yes? *(Pause.)* What's that then, Greenham Common?

Mel: Well, um, er, it's like a big shopping precinct, isn't it? Like Brent Cross.

Griff: What? I thought it was more of a nuclear thing, you know? I thought it was nuclear.

Mel: Yeah, well obviously, it's nuclear as well. But there is a big shopping precinct there. So what you can do, right, is you can go down in the car and you can park the car up, and leave the kids in the crèche, then you can go and do your nuclear business, and then you can get the shopping for the whole week.

Griff: Well, that's marvellous, isn't it?

Mel: Very clever idea. I mean, that's why it's taken off ...

Griff: Why do they call it the women's peace movement there, then?

Mel: Well, how the bloody hell should I know, I've only been a feminist for five minutes. How do I know what's going on in a bloody woman's mind?

Griff: Well, why do they call it, then, I thought you'd be able to tell me, why they call it the women's peace movement?

Mel: It's obvious, isn't it? All the women, they go down to Greenham Common, and we get some peace.

●

Christina Dodwell is a very resourceful woman. She is an explorer who has travelled in many wild places. Sometimes she goes on foot, at other times on the back of an elephant, and occasionally aboard something as modern as a small plane. Often she goes alone on her expeditions, but she had a companion – Lesley, a nurse from New Zealand – when travelling in Africa. They became the first women to paddle down the Congo in a dugout canoe.

The canoeing trip was just one of the exploits outlined in Gavin Scott's *Profile of Christina Dodwell* on Radio 4. Paddling a canoe in the Congo is beset with certain dangers, as you can imagine, among them the presence of cannibals.

Christina Dodwell: Well, I'm very slow often to realize these things because – I mean, it doesn't really matter to me what people eat. I'm interested in it as far as diet goes, yes. The cannibals are easier to recognize in Africa because they sharpen their teeth to points. But I'd been through tribes with single fang points and double fang points before I even realized that this was a cannibal trait.

Gavin Scott: How did the people whom you met in the villages on the Congo react to you?

It's a super recipe. I picked up in Africa...

Christina Dodwell: Oh, we would climb ashore and find this group of people gathering and they'd stand there and just look with – their expressions were wonderful because they'd be incredulous, afraid, the children often would scream and run to hide behind their mothers' legs and they'd peer out through grass skirts at us. All these little eyes. And we'd step forward to shake hands with the men because, although shaking hands is probably a custom that they'd never used or had, it is still an important contact, good will. You know, it shows, where you don't have a language in common, it's definitely a way of communicating. And usually in the background I'd hear arguments between women, and one could hear them saying – although of course in their own language, 'They're not women', 'I tell you they're women', 'They can't be women', 'They've got to be women', 'They look like –', 'They're not women'; and this would be going on, and finally they'd realize that we were women.

Gavin Scott: Was the fact that you were women a difficulty, do you think, or did it help when you were meeting strange tribes, on the river, people who didn't know you, and to whom you were completely vulnerable?

Christina Dodwell: I think it does both. It's unhelpful in that, being a woman, one clearly is at a disadvantage, but it's also, I think, tremendously helpful because a woman doesn't symbolize any kind of a threat, whereas men can be seen as threatening. Who's going to be afraid, really, of women? And I always felt that this acted on my behalf.

Gavin Scott: On the other hand women have occasion, reason, to be afraid themselves. Did you have to repel many advances from people that you met in the course of your journeys?

Christina Dodwell: We developed all these curious ways of repelling the advances, because, yes, they would always come, people will always ask. And so long as they take the 'no's with good grace this is all right. Sometimes, as we got further down the river, and the land was more populated, young men would paddle out in their canoes to ask us if we – 'Good morning. Would you like sex. I see you don't have a man with you. Can we offer you satisfaction?' So, you know, we'd say no. But – to avoid them getting even as far as asking – if we just stared straight ahead, rather blankly, paddled in unison, and sang dirges, this terrified people because they thought we weren't real.

Gavin Scott: A funeral march, sort of thing.

Christina Dodwell: Yes, yes, and they didn't proposition us that way.

●

We have been led to believe that the sex lives of the Victorians were rather austere. No nice woman was thought to enjoy sex; she performed it as a duty. 'Think of England,' she was told – or so we have laughingly assumed. But BBC2's history programme *Timewatch* uncovered some new research about the Victorians which could well dispel these misconceptions about our ancestors.

Professor Peter Gay, who had done the research for the programme, concluded that the Victorians, though they may have been prudish enough to cover the table legs lest they should arouse passion, were very probably having a high old time of it behind their lace net curtains.

By way of illustration, John Tusa, who presents *Timewatch*, produced the diary of a Massachusetts housewife of the period. Mable Loomis Todd was the lively and vivacious wife of Mr David Todd, who became the

31

Director of Amherst College in 1881. What sort of headmaster he was we may never know, but we do know quite a lot about his sex life because his wife recorded it in her diary.

Reader: On the morning of 15 May my darling and I came up from breakfast and had a very beautiful few minutes of love in our room. Every night he undressed me on the bright Turkey rug before the fire and then wrapped me up to keep me warm. Then he took me in his arms and tucked me safely in bed and kissed me – over and over. We retired at 7 and had a magnificent evening, David and I. I shall never forget it, so I'll not write about it.

John Tusa: The entry is followed by two symbols that indicate they made love twice that night. But David Todd was not the only man in Mabel's life; her lover was the leading man in Amherst, Austin Dickinson. He was older than her, married, with grown-up children. This intense affair lasted for nearly fifteen years, until Dickinson's death in 1895. Surprisingly, although her husband knew about the affair, he connived in it, perhaps because it covered his own infidelities. The affair was well known in Amherst society but it did not make Mabel a social outcast. Her diaries are filled with entries like 'Austin this evening'. And at the same time invitations to the most select social occasions. She played a very prominent role in Amherst society, even setting up in the town a branch of the notoriously conservative Daughters of the American Revolution.

But such sexual enjoyment in marriage was not confined to the American middle class. The Liberal Prime Minister Gladstone was an earnest prayerful Christian with a severe conscience. His diaries, written in political London and here at his private house at Hawarden, near Chester, where he was married, touch on every aspect of his life. His relationship with his wife Catherine is dealt with in detail.

Gladstone's first child, William, was born on 3 June 1840. Gladstone witnessed the labour: 'Catherine awakened me and sent for Dr Locock. The whole day was consumed in a slow but favourable labour, till 11.00 the pains were slight, till 3 quite ineffectual, about 7.30 they began to assume the expulsory character. Praise and thanks be to God for the fortitude He gives her.'

Late in October 1842, shortly after her second child was born, Catherine Gladstone developed difficulties with the flow of her milk – a difficulty which persisted over the next ten years. Gladstone's diaries record his constant awareness of his wife's problem and his own role in helping her overcome it. 'C. was in the meshes of her old difficulties today – much rubbing by Mrs Smith and me seemed to keep the right organ from getting into an obstinate state.'

Mr Gladstone was more than what we think of as the typical Victorian. He was a man of strong and open feelings about his wife's body. The Victorians may have been closed; they were not less complex. Gladstone's response to his wife's difficult labour is entirely modern in its feelings and vocabulary. 'Today all is smooth and happy, the child vigorous and very sweet-tempered, Catherine in the best possible state of body and absolutely melted in the penetrating sense of maternal love and delight. But she allows the pain was awful.'

●

A sympathetic husband is a valuable asset to any woman but particularly if she is someone in the public eye. On BBC1 the series *The Other Half* focused on the less well-known partner in a marriage or relationship.

Mrs Edwina Currie is the Conservative Member of Parliament for Derbyshire South. Her other half is her husband, Ray. John Pitman followed her as she kept to her busy schedule of constituency visits and parliamentary duties along with minding her family. Her husband has been very important in helping to further her political ambitions.

Edwina Currie: Right at the beginning of my attempts to get into Parliament I was on the short short-list, that's the last three, for a big by-election up north. And I didn't get it. But I've always been determined to learn from everything that I don't do very well. So, afterwards I rang up the senior agent of the party, who'd been there, and I said to him, What did I do wrong – you know, can you give me some tips? And he said to me, Oh, well it wasn't you at all. You were fine, don't change anything, he said, but ... I don't know what your relationship with your husband is like but I would suggest you have a word with him. And I said, Why, what did he do? And he said, Well, when you were speaking and answering questions, he was looking out the window, looking at the ceiling, looking at the audience and looking at his hands; he was doing everything except look at you. What he ought to do, and what you're going to have to tell him to do, is look in total adoration at your left ear 'ole the whole time you are talking ... and not budge his eyes from you. So I said, Yes, I see. And he came home and I told him and he was speechless for three days. But he's been doing it ever since.

Ray Currie: I wasn't impressed at all. I'd had a long train journey on a hot day to get up there and had tried very, very hard – and all I got was a lecture for it, as if I'd been responsible.

John Pitman: Did you have a row about it?

Ray Currie: No. I probably left the house in the direction of the pub fairly swiftly after she'd passed the message on, I think.

Woman: Gets her name in the paper more than Elizabeth Taylor.

Woman: ... She couldn't do it, with a young family, without the support of her husband. I mean, he's been absolutely marvellous. You know. He's in the background all the time ... just like Denis Thatcher, I think. It's unlikely that Denis Thatcher would ever be caught carrying the boss's handbag, but then Ray is a new boy to the game, despite the fact that he and Edwina are already being called the next Margaret and Denis.

Ray Currie: I find it very very flattering. Obviously it's flattering as far as she's concerned ... and from the political angle. But also ... if in terms of the sort of small political life that we lead I can do it one quarter as well as he does ... and put up with something which we're preserved from, which is a sort of public teasing, if you like, then I would be very happy.

Edwina Currie: What shall I show you? Have you seen the photo of Daddy?

Susie Currie: I see you and Daddy. Kissing as well. What does it say?

Edwina Currie: Read it out.

Susie Currie: Triumphant South Derbyshire Tory, Mrs Edwina Currie, gets a hug and kiss from husband Ray.

Edwina Currie: He didn't know he was being photographed, did he?

Ray Currie: I remember, I not only knew I was being photographed but they asked us to do it again.

Edwina Currie: They asked us to do it again, that's right.

Ray Currie: . . . Sounds familiar.

Susie Currie: Why on earth do they put it in the paper?

Edwina Currie: Well, why not? Some of the things I get up to are news.

Susie Currie: Mummy – found it!

Edwina Currie: Found what? 'Squatting at the House of Commons by office-less MPs is getting out of hand. You will recall that I reported impressive new Tory Edwina Currie bagging the nearest office, contrary to tradition' – it wasn't an office, it was only a desk – 'the moment she arrived at the House.' And I discover another Tory, Stephen Norris, has done the same. I'm not surprised because I went to school with him. Let's have a look at this one. Those are called economic indicators and you won't be able to under– You'll have to do economics . . .

Susie Currie: It says labour there.

Edwina Currie: Yes, but it's a different kind of labour. That's people who work.

Susie Currie: 'Prime Minister and Mr Denis Thatcher request the honour of the company of Mrs Edwina Currie and Mr' – is that you? – 'Mr Raymond Currie . . .'

Edwina Currie: Who's Denis Thatcher?

Susie Currie: Mrs Thatcher's wife, of course.

Edwina Currie: Mrs Thatcher's what?

Susie Currie: I mean husband.

Edwina Currie: Husband, that's right.

●

Mr Thatcher's wife tried her hand at acting this year. It was when she was called upon to present an award on behalf of the Viewers and Listeners Association to the television series *Yes, Minister.*

Yes, Minister gives an inside picture of the workings of government with the fictional MP, Jim Hacker, constantly fencing with his senior civil servants. Whenever the Prime Minister is referred to, it is always carefully phrased so as not to indicate whether it is a man or a woman. Our woman Prime Minister, however, is a great fan of the series and she decided that the award-presentation ceremony would be a very good moment to get in on the act. She wrote herself a *Yes, (Prime) Minister* sketch in which the PM comes out of the shadows and is face to face with Paul Eddington as Jim Hacker and Nigel Hawthorne as Sir Humphrey Appleby. The performance was recorded and broadcast on *The World at One*.

Prime Minister: Ah, good morning, Jim, Sir Humphrey. Do come in and sit down. How's your wife? Is she well?

Jim Hacker (puzzled): Oh yes, fine, Prime Minister. Fine. Thank you. Yes, fine.

Prime Minister: Good. So pleased. I've been meaning to have a word with you for some time. I've got an idea.

Jim Hacker (brightening visibly): An idea, Prime Minister? Oh good.

Sir Humphrey (guardedly): An idea, Prime Minister?

Prime Minister: Well, not really an idea. I've done quite a bit of thinking and I'm sure you, Jim, are quite the man to carry it out. It's got to do with a kind of institution and you are sort of responsible for institutions, aren't you?

Sir Humphrey (cautiously): Institutions, Prime Minister?

Jim Hacker (decisively): Oh yes, institutions fall to me. Most definitely. And you want me to set one up, I suppose?

Prime Minister: Set one up? Certainly not. I want you to get rid of one.

Jim Hacker (astonished): Get rid of one, Prime Minister?

Prime Minister: Yes. It's all very simple. I want you to abolish economists.

Jim Hacker (mouth open): Abolish economists, Prime Minister?

Prime Minister: Yes, abolish economists – quickly.

Sir Humphrey (silkily): All of them, Prime Minister?

Prime Minister: Yes, all of them. They never agree on anything. They just fill the heads of politicians with all sorts of curious notions, like the more you spend, the richer you get.

Jim Hacker (coming round to the idea): I take your point, Prime Minister. Can't have the nation's time wasted on curious notions, can we? No.

Sir Humphrey (sternly): Minister.

Prime Minister: Quite right, Jim. Absolute waste of time. Simply got to go.

Jim Hacker (uncertain): Simply got to go?

Prime Minister (motherly): Yes, Jim. Don't worry. If it all goes wrong, I shall get the blame. But if it goes right – as it will – then you'll get the credit for redeploying a lot of misapplied resources. Probably get promotion too.

Sir Humphrey (indignantly): Resources? Resources, Prime Minister? Surely we're talking about economists.

Prime Minister: Were, Sir Humphrey. Were.

Jim Hacker (decisively): Yes, Humphrey, were. We're going to get rid of them.

Prime Minister: Well, it's all settled then. I'll look forward to receiving your plan for abolition soon. Tomorrow, shall we say? I'd like you to announce it before it all leaks.

Jim Hacker (brightly): Tomorrow then, Prime Minister.

Prime Minister: Yes, well, sort it out. Now, Sir Humphrey – what did you say your degree was?

Sir Humphrey (innocently): Degree, Prime Minister?

Prime Minister (firmly): Yes, Sir Humphrey, degree. Your degree. You have one, I take it – most permanent secretaries do – or perhaps two.

Sir Humphrey (modestly): Er, well actually, Prime Minister, a double first.

Prime Minister: Congratulations, Sir Humphrey, but what in?

Sir Humphrey (weakly): Politics – er ... and er ... economics.

Prime Minister (soothingly): Capital, my dear Sir Humphrey. You'll know exactly where to start.

Sir Humphrey (bleakly): Yes, Prime Minister.

Exit Jim Hacker and Sir Humphrey.

●

The royal family are the next candidates for a radio sketch. Ray Gosling found this scene in *Punch* when he was reviewing the weekly magazines for the Radio 4 programme *News Stand*. The scene takes place during the last war.

Act II, Scene 1. Inside Buckingham Palace. Present are King George VI, Queen Elizabeth, the two princesses and the Prime Minister.

Churchill: With gracious permission, I should like to sing your Majesty a little song.

The King: Must you?

Churchill: Don't have your daughter knitting comforts for the servicemen,
Don't give her shirts to stitch and press.
As our future radiant Queen she should grace the war machine –
Put her in the ATS.

Princess Elizabeth claps her hands delightedly and sings:
I'll get grease upon my clothes and I'll learn some frightful oaths,
And I'll pick up dreadful habits in the mess,
But I really must be seen to be part of the machine –
Put me in the ATS.

A chorus of ladies-in-waiting prances across the stage singing:
Put her in the ATS.

38

Princess Margaret Rose skips into the spotlight.

Margaret: I'm a little passion flower,
          Growing wilder every hour.
          Mr Churchill hear my plea:
          What about the Wrens for me?
          Toora-loora-loora-lee.

She puts the tip of one finger on top of her head and pirouettes.

The Queen: That will do, child. You have delighted us enough.

●

Robert Lacey's theme for his BBC2 series *Aristocrats* was the other royal houses of Europe.

Among the countries he visited that still have royal families was the tiny principality of Liechtenstein, whose reigning Prince is Franz Josef II. He and his family live in grand style surrounded by rich tapestries and fine paintings. Franz Josef's wife, the Princess Gina, claimed, though, to have simple tastes.

Princess Gina: No, I don't feel like a rich person, I don't. Well, I don't feel like it. I don't know. What a question! I haven't got a helicopter, I haven't got a yacht, I haven't got horses, I haven't got a Rolls Royce, and I don't miss it.

Robert Lacey: You'd never like to have any of those things?

Princess Gina: Not really, funnily enough, no.

Robert Lacey: But you could afford to have those things?

Princess Gina: I don't think anybody ever in our family thought of having that sort of thing, and I don't. We've got a lot of responsibilities. I mean, this talk about being one of the richest families, that's always – I find these, what do you call them, adjectives, always wrong because you can't eat a painting and you can't make clothes out of a castle. I mean, what is rich?

Robert Lacey: Rich is buying yourself a country.

In 1712 Johan Adam from Liechtenstein paid 290 thousand florins for some poor and flood-prone farming land around the village of Vaduz and he amalgamated it with neighbouring lands whose title deeds he held already. The land itself promised little revenue, and Liechtenstein scarcely needed yet another medieval castle, but it did carry an ancient entitlement to the status of Prince and it was the title that Johan Adam paid for. The off-the-peg principality was renamed Liechtenstein, Europe's only state to carry the name of its ruling family.

Princess Nora of Liechtenstein clearly appreciated the lifestyle her father's position had assured for her. Sitting within sneezing distance of a beautiful Rembrandt portrait, she told Robert Lacey what it meant to be brought up in a royal palace.

Princess Nora: I think it's very nice because we see nice things every day and one gets used to looking at beautiful things.

Robert Lacey: Did you realize how valuable they were?

Princess Nora: I think when I was little I realized it very quickly because when we were small my father hardly ever screamed at us, but every now and then he used, when we started throwing things in here, for example if there was a certain possibility that

we miss and hit the Rembrandt – I remember we owned a painting by Leonardo. When it wasn't down in the museum, it was – somewhere stored away here. I remember holding it and showing it to friends. Then it was sold to Washington – wasn't it the sixties? When I was living in Washington I went to see it, and there it was in this little room – in a little room of its own with all the sorts of lights on it, and I was just standing in that room sort of looking at it and said, Well, there it ended up, and I had it, held and I was –

Robert Lacey: Holding it?

Princess Nora: Yes.

●

For those of us not born with a silver spoon in our mouth this is much more the sort of thing we are likely to encounter in our daily lives:

I never had a piece of toast particularly long and wide
But fell upon the sanded floor and *always* on the buttered side.

●

That, as I am sure you will recognize, is an illustration of a phenomenon known as Murphy's Law, a fragment I picked up from *Science Through the Looking-Glass* on Radio 4. Was it Murphy who was responsible for a bad tea harvest which is likely to raise the price of our national drink? Who can tell? At any rate, the news prompted the topical comedy programme *Weekending* to dash off an 'Ode to a Tea Leaf'. It was addressed to the late Poet Laureate, Sir John Betjeman, and written in his style by Alexander Gleason.

Do you recall, do you recall, the old year '83?
When you sat down for a teabreak, and there actually was tea.
Strolling down to Tesco, expectation curled the lips,
The lure of Tetley teabags, the draw of PG Tips.

Oh, the Lapsang I once slurped in Balham, the Darjeeling I
    spilt on Joan's dress,
Will the Earl Gray 'ere flow, as it did years ago, at my semi in
    Shoeberryness?

41

Oh, Joan, can I ever forget you, on that day when you
  promised to serve,
When I whipped out my quick-boiling kettle
And you gave me your Twinings Reserve?

Drinking char on the patio, eating scones upon the lawn,
In those golden days of '83 before the tea had gorn.
Now when 'tis time for tiffin, at my place in north west three,
There's just rotten bread and butter, and UH bloody T.

•

As you might imagine, the Spanish avant-garde film director Don Luis
Buñuel demanded something a little stronger than a cup of tea.

The *Arena* programme on BBC2 presented an appreciation of his work.
Buñuel was a surrealist. In the twenties he collaborated with Salvador Dali.
His films were very strange. For me, they created an atmosphere that
lingers in the mind long after I have forgotten what the story was supposed
to be about.

His subject matter offended a lot of people. He was thought to be
subversive and blasphemous. Considering that he was brought up in
Catholic Spain at the beginning of this century, it was perhaps rather
surprising that blasphemous language was common currency with him.
He could not avoid it even when doing something as simple as giving his
recipe for making a dry martini.

When it comes to drinks, red wine is my favourite, but it does
nothing for the imagination.

To provoke, or sustain, a reverie in a bar, you have to drink
English gin, especially in the form of the dry martini. The dry
martini is composed essentially of gin and a few drops of Noilly
Prat. Connoisseurs who like their martinis very dry maintain that
it's enough merely to pass the bottle of Noilly Prat through a ray
of sunlight before the light hits the glass of gin.

They used to have a saying in America that the perfect dry
martini should resemble the Annunciation – the moment when
the Virgin Mary conceived. For, according to St Thomas
Aquinas, the generative power of the Holy Ghost pierced the
Virgin's hymen 'like a ray of sunlight passes through a window
without breaking it'.

But all this seems a trifle excessive to me.

42

For those who are still with me, let me give you my personal recipe.

Keep all the ingredients – the gin, the glasses and the shaker – chilled until ready to serve. Pour a few drops of Noilly Prat over the ice and then a few drops of Angostura bitters, stir it, then pour it away, keeping only the ice, which retains a faint taste of both. Pour straight gin over the ice, stir it again and serve.

●

That's not the sort of drink you would get at the Radio 3 wine bar, Heyday's, featured in what must be the nearest thing Radio 3 has come to a strip cartoon. The author is Chris Miller.

Mr Heyday presides behind the bar, keeping an observant eye on the daily parade of customers and giving us, the listeners, a wry rundown on what he is really thinking about them as they knock back their Heyday's Rather Decent Ordinary Claret.

In an episode called 'Ladies Last' we find him watching a group of mostly elderly women dancing in a feverish circle. They are the celebrated Greenham Grannies, who a short while back set up a GLC-sponsored peace camp in London. One of them is a customer of his, Peggy Pepper.

Peggy: Aye-aye, Mr Heyday!

Heyday: Hello, Peggy!

Four hundred years ago, these women would have been witches. But today they are less forbidding – no longer infernal murderous hags, but gentle vegetarians. It does make a difference ...

Peggy (coming on and going off again, as if moving in a circle):
Double, double, toil and trouble,
Wheatgerm makes the cauldron bubble ...

Second woman (ditto):
Fillet of a lentil steak,
Brown rice, kelp and carrot cake ...

Third woman (ditto):
Soya newt and soya frog,
Soya bat and soya dog ...

Peggy (ditto):
Lots of bran and prunes and fibre
Keep you healthy up the Khyber ...

(Coming on): Rhiannon be with you, Mr Heyday. And with thy spirit.

Heyday: Thank you very much. Are you coming in for a drink?

Peggy: She wills it, so I come.

Heyday: Peggy sits at the bar and I pour her a macrobiotic Corsican red made entirely from recycled kidney beans. She is, as you may have guessed, going through a religious phase.

Peggy: To the Great Goddess of Earth, the Mother of Us All!

Heyday: God is female, is she, Peggy?

Peggy: How could she be anything else?

Heyday: Have you noticed how women everywhere are muscling in on religion? Kaye Barber, who you met just now, is a member of a sisters' collective that has set itself the task of rewriting the entire Judaeo-Christian myth from a feminist standpoint. No, really. In their version of Genesis, Chapter 3, Eve no longer gives Adam the apple. She gives him the raspberry. But Peggy, I think, is decidedly more radical.

44

Peggy: The world and the human race have been in decline since the advent of patriarchy five millennia ago. Before then, the earth was a place of unbridled joy, watched over by the Great Goddess, variously called Isis ... Gaia ... Ashtoreth ... Dana ... Rhiannon ... Ishtar ... Cerridwen ... Cybele –

Heyday: Peggy!

Peggy: Peggy? Yes – why not?

●

Always wishing to be the first with important news, the *Today* programme broke this story to a waking nation. Peter Hobday and John Timpson were presenting the programme that day and it fell to the senior man, Timpson, to make this momentous announcement.

John Timpson: The award for the best public lavatory in the country has just been made: the Golden Loo Award – for the place just next to St Paul's Church in Covent Garden, which sounds quite fantastic. They have pictures of tranquil country scenes on the pink walls of the Ladies; the Gents is painted blue and decorated with sporting prints of old yachting scenes. Both have pot plants, hanging baskets of plastic flowers, china clowns; women have expensively perfumed soaps and fluffy handtowels. And the quote of the week, I think, came from one of the splendid men who keep these places. It says: 'Women spend a lot of time in here. Sometimes they bring their kids in and dance to the music. They recommend us to their mates. On Saturdays there are enormous queues outside. I don't know how they can wait so long.' Full marks to Mr Bedwell and his colleague up there in St Paul's. They're doing a great job.

Peter Hobday: If you want to know exactly what the award is – it's a mahogany lavatory seat trimmed with gold braid.

●

Sir Robin Day with his spotted bow ties and gruff manner is now something of an institution. He has been in television for nearly thirty years. In the fifties for ITN and the BBC he helped to form a style of interviewing that many now copy. When Sir Robin took part in *The Levin Interviews* on BBC2, Bernard Levin went so far as to suggest that he had invented the modern form of political interview. Taking the compliment in his stride, Sir Robin went on to express his concern about the power of the medium he had helped to shape. Television, he said, has an appetite for violence; and he believes that television reporting in some cases has contributed to the spread of unreason and violence.

Robin Day: I think our presentation of news and events has been affected by television's appetite for violence and action. Our news bulletins have become too much a kaleidoscope of happenings and visual happenings rather than explanations of issues – not always, but I think that has been the tendency. One simple example: a politician addresses a speech, a meeting – let's say, about the Common Market. It's broken up by a bunch of extremists, a dozen of them at the back. Television may not always ... but I've seen this. The politician speaks; he's summarized in a couple of sentences over shots of the hall; but the real sound and the action is the people being thrown out, because that's a minute's sexy film. Now people have begun to learn about this and they've begun to play it down a bit, but the danger's always there. Take a thing like the Nigerian civil war. Now television showed pictures of the starving Biafran babies – I'm not taking sides in that war now; that's irrelevant – but it was very, very difficult indeed to give any television balance to the pictures of the starving babies, yet there was an argument on the other side: that you didn't want to break up a great nation and Balkanize Africa. But you try doing a sexy television item. When I say sexy, I don't mean sexy; I mean impact-making. You try doing a dramatic or exciting item on the Balkanization of Africa – it has to be a discussion of some kind. Yet I say those in charge of television must restrain themselves from using the power of television solely to project the visual aspects of world affairs, because the most important things are not always visual. If the President is shot, that is visual and very important, but the factors and the issues and the explanations are often much more important than things you can see.

Bernard Levin: Well, you see, you said in the course of that that it's television's appetite for violence, etc. ... Isn't it *our* appetite for violence, the people's attitude to violence, the *viewers'*, because television, like newspapers, will not long survive if it gives its customers something they don't want? Or do you not

46

agree, do you think that television in that sense has a duty to, not just to inform, which it obviously has, to educate, but to, as it were, direct public taste, public attitudes, public things, all that? At any rate, even if it doesn't have a duty to do it, that's what it does, and it can lead them downwards as well as upwards.

Robin Day: I don't think it should direct public taste but I do think those in charge of television should try to put its power on behalf, on the side of reason. I think they should try to restrain the capacity of television to encourage unreason and what I think Bertrand Russell called 'the anti-rational philosophy of the naked will', and I think that television could do a great deal of good by redressing the balance, because we don't want our society to slide into violence and unreason. In your question you raised the question of don't the public want this – well, that doesn't interest me in the slightest. I mean, the public would flock in their thousands to see a public execution, but as a society we don't allow it. The public would love to read reports of divorce cases, they are not allowed by law – except the judge's conclusions. So I think as a civilized society we take decisions which will not pander to the lowest instincts of human nature.

●

If there is a public appetite for watching violence, it was certainly not pandered to at the time of the Falklands war. It was some weeks before we saw television pictures of the fighting, pictures which gave an idea of the sufferings and deaths of 'our boys' who had made such a fine show sailing out of Portsmouth.

One of the fatalities in the war in the South Atlantic was Lieutenant David Tinker. Just two days before hostilities ceased, his ship, HMS *Glamorgan*, was struck by an Exocet missile which killed thirteen members of her crew.

Lieutenant Tinker's father, Hugh Tinker, is a retired professor of politics at Lancaster University. He had been in close touch with his son through letters ever since the start of the campaign. Professor Tinker decided that his monument to his son's memory would be a published collection of those letters. The result was a book called *A Message from the Falklands.*

For *The World This Weekend* on Radio 4, Neil Bennett looked through the letters and talked to Hugh Tinker about them. The correspondence did not reflect the conventional views of a serving officer blindly going off to war to serve his country right or wrong. They began cheerfully enough on 2 April 1982, the day the Argentinians invaded.

47

Reader: Thank you for your letter. This is just a quick one to say that today we have heard the news that we are off to bash the Argentinians. This is great fun and very much like Maggie Thatcher to stick up for our remaining colonies with a show of force. Of course, the whole thing may blow over in a week, but the thrill of some real confrontation away from the nuclear bombs of the northern world in a colonial war is quite exciting compared to the usual dull routine of exercises and paperwork.

Neil Bennett: But only eight days later David Tinker's letters are raising precisely the same questions being asked back home, about the rationale behind the looming confrontation.

Reader: At times the situation seems so absolutely silly. Here we are in 1982, fighting a colonial war on the other side of the world; 28,000 men going to fight over a fairly dreadful piece of land inhabited by 1800 people. After it's all over and millions of pounds have been expended they'll be left in peace, having had their homes destroyed by shelling, and the 28,000 will go away again. Moreover, one side – Britain – has supplied the other with its weapons, so that the war can be started in the first place, and both sides will end up impoverished.

Neil Bennett: By 22 May, *Glamorgan* had been under bombardment for days in the waters off Port Stanley, but when she was moved briefly out of the most dangerous area, David had the time to reply to a letter from his father.

Reader: Your long, marvellous letter of 6 May arrived today. It was like a breath of sanity coming into this totally mad world here. I'm glad that you think that way about Mrs Thatcher and the war, as I have come to think since this business started. I sometimes wonder if I'm totally odd in that I utterly oppose all this killing that is going on over a flag. Wilfred Owen wrote that 'There'll come a day when men make war on death for lives, not men for flags', but it has been the reverse here.

Neil Bennett: David Tinker clearly wasn't cast in the normal military mould. His letters question the wisdom of fighting over the Falklands issue; he bemoans the lack of early-warning air-cover to protect the fleet; he asks what'll happen to the Falklands if Britain *does* win. If they're to be turned into a garrison, he argues, it'll show the complete hypocrisy of the British government, which was going to leave the islands undefended. Above all, he's highly sceptical of the principle for which they were supposed to be fighting, and for which he eventually lost his life. His words are an indictment of politicians everywhere, and they make increasingly bitter reading. But with the benefit of four months' hindsight, what does David's father, Hugh, make of the Falklands conflict? Does he think there was a principle worth fighting for?

Hugh Tinker: I find it very difficult to answer that. I don't think that his life was lived in vain because fortunately he did leave these amazing letters, which I hope will show people very clearly how one man refused to accept anything but the truth. The principle is frankly beyond me. We went to fight aggression – yes, that was good. But let us remember that only a few months beforehand it had been decided to abandon all our defences in the South Atlantic; we really invited the Argentinians to walk in and they accepted the invitation. Having done that, of course, then the decision was taken that they must be thrown out using the whole might of the British Navy. In the process of this campaign the Royal Navy has suffered appalling losses; the extent of these losses I don't think is fully realized by the public. And now we have taken on this extraordinary commitment in which a sizable part of our forces are going to be locked up in an area of the world where we really have no national interest whatsoever. So that the principle behind this just escapes me.

Neil Bennett: It's Hugh Tinker's belief that the commitment to defend the Falklands won't be indefinite, despite what the Defence Minister, Mr Nott, had to say when he visited the islands. Meanwhile, they have to come to terms with the loss of their son in a way which neither they nor he believed in. How, then, had they possibly been able to cope with those scenes of rejoicing when the ones who did survive were welcomed home?

Hugh Tinker: The first thing is that you very quickly learn that you shouldn't be sorry that other people were saved. It didn't really make us unhappy to see the soldiers and sailors coming back; it made us feel happy because they at any rate were safe. Yes, of course it was dreadful when eventually we went down to *Glamorgan* and we saw the flight deck where the Exocet had hit, and the destruction that'd been caused. Of course it was dreadful, and of course we mourn. But, as I say, our other feeling was of gladness that other mothers and fathers didn't lose their sons.

●

The Falkland Islands are one of the last outposts of the British Empire. At one time England's sons were dispatched to many a far-flung corner of the world to keep the flag flying. The brightest jewel in the imperial crown was India, and to look after its many facets whole armies of civil servants, soldiers, public officials and their wives were sent there from the mother country. Voices from the last days of the Raj were assembled by Christopher Cook for a programme about British India on BBC2.

Iris Portal was a child when her father became settlement officer in the state of Kotta in Rajputana. It was a happy time for her and she revelled in her Indian childhood, but then, like all English girls in India, she had to come home to England for her schooling. It was not until she was seventeen that her mother came to fetch her back to India. Her father's career had prospered and he had become Secretary to the Education Department of the Government of India. This meant that Iris Portal could be launched with some style into British Indian society. It was all clearly enormous fun for her, although there were certain rules to abide by.

We were never allowed to go out alone with a man to dinner or dance, so you always had to be in a party and you were supposed to have a married woman in the party. I mean, my parents would never have let me go out to dinner in a party of young men and women without a married woman. Well, a married woman was very likely a very lively one who may have been ... had quite shaky morals – but she was a married woman.

Girls were never seduced in that society. There was plenty of adultery going on, very discreet and rather more elegantly done than nowadays. Such a lot of separation, you see, in Indian marriages between husbands and wives, and in many, many cases the greatest possible happiness and faithfulness – but there were ... it was not easy to maintain a very ... absolutely snowy-pure life in that sort of world. But girls were not seduced. It wouldn't have done at all. You see, we all knew each other very well. Everyone really knew something about everyone else and there was no pill or anything like that. I mean, you really couldn't take these risks. There was quite a lot of – I don't care for the expression 'petting', but there it was. Can't think quite how else to put it. And dances ... at dances there were discreet little curtained-off corners by palms and pots of rhododendrons, and things called 'caller jaggers', which means dark place. And if you were very much ... having a sort of affair with some beautiful young man, you did rather make for the caller jaggers, but ... nothing much more than that. To my mind, it was immensely romantic to go home from the dance in your rickshaw after tremendous waltzing and polkaing about the whole evening, lovely music. Huge enormous moon, you see, Indian moon, and bright twinkling stars and Himalayas in the distance, and this ... They were so good-looking, all those men – they were men of course, not boys. And they were beautifully dressed always, and you know it does knock a girl awfully, those lovely clothes, it really does, I think still. And they walked beside you in the rickshaw holding your hand over the hood. The *gemparnies* immensely discreet – anyway they thought we were all mad – and instead of having to run like mad home, they just had a nice easy walk, so they were quite happy. And you murmured away and looked at the moon, and so on.

●

Regular listeners to *Pick of the Week* will know that one of my hobbies is enjoying and learning about wine. Wine drinking in this country is on the increase and, according to Kingsley Amis, in the future there may be even more wine buffs than there are now.

Amis's short story *The 2003 Claret*, broadcast on Radio 3, tells of a time traveller called Simpson who is transported to the year 2010 to see what life will be like then. His brief is to observe fashion and behaviour, but particularly, since he works for a wine firm, to sample the wines. His director has every confidence in him as a man ideally suited for the job in hand – for the balding, fortyish Mr Simpson has been invested as a Knight of Bordeaux and has made claret his special study.

Simpson is duly shot forward in time and lands inconspicuously in Hyde Park, a lump of gold in his pocket to pawn for currency. At the end of his day in the year 2010, he decides that he had better concentrate on the serious business of drinking, and so he goes into a bar. A waiter approaches – and this is where the director's confidence in Simpson's taste buds is put to the test.

He enjoyed claret all right, but he also enjoyed other French wines, and German wines, and Italian wines, and Iberian wines, and Balkan wines, and fortified wines, and spirits, and liqueurs,

51

and *apéritifs*, and cocktails, and draught beer, and bottled beer, and stout, and cider, and perry – all the way down to Fernet Branca. (There were some drinks he had never drunk – *arak*, *kava*, Gumpoldskirchener Rotgipfler, methylated spirits – but they were getting fewer all the time.) Anyway, feeling dehydrated after his walk round the streets he, unreflecting, ordered a pint of bitter.

'I'm sorry, monsieur, I don't understand. What is this bitter?'

'Bitter beer, ale; you know. Haven't you got any?'

'Beer, monsieur?' The waiter's voice rose in contempt. '*Beer?* I'm afraid you're in the wrong district for that.'

Several men turned round, nudged one another and stared at Simpson, who blushed and said, 'Well ... a glass of wine, then.'

'France, Germany, Luxembourg, Austria ...?'

Simpson tried to think. 'A claret, please. Let's say – a nice Saint-Emilion.'

'Château Le Couvent, Château Puy Blanquet, Château Belle-fore Belcier, Château Grand-Corbin-Despagne ...'

'Oh ... I leave it to you.'

'Bien, monsieur. And the year? Will you leave that to me too?'

'If you don't mind.'

The waiter swept away. Conscious that all eyes were upon him, Simpson tried to sink into his chair. Before he could compose himself, a middle-aged man from a nearby table had come over and sat down next to him. 'Well, who are you?' this man asked.

'A – a traveller. From Sydney.'

'These days that's no excuse for not knowing your wines, friend. Some of them Rubicons and Malbecs are as firm and fully rounded as all bar the greatest Burgundies. And I found a Barossa Riesling on holiday this year that was pretty near as gay as Kreuznacher Steinweg. You well up on the Barossas, friend?'

'No, not really, I'm afraid.'

'Thought not, somehow. Otherwise you wouldn't stalk in here and screech out for *beer*. Ger, ought to be ashamed of yourself, you ought.'

'I'm awfully sorry.'

'Should hope so and all. Now, I'm an honest working man, see. I'm a DRIP, I am.'

'A drip?'

'Domestic Reactor Installation Patentee. Don't they go in for them down under? Now you listen to me. When I come in here to

52

meet my colleagues and crack a bottle or two after the daily round, I don't want my palate soured by some toff yelling out about beer, especially not when we got a really elegant Gevrey-Chambertin or Chambolle-Musigny or something of that in front of us. It's psychosomatic, like. Just the idea of beer's enough to cut off some of the subtler overtones, get me?'

'I'm sorry,' Simpson said again. 'I didn't realize. But tell me: don't you eat while you're drinking these wines?'

'What, and foul up the taste buds with fat and sauces and muck? You got a nerve even mentioning food in a place like this. We're oenophiles in here, I'll have you know, not a bunch of pigs. Ah, here's your claret.' The stranger held the glass up to the light, then sniffed it delicately. 'Right, now let's see what you've got to say about this. And get on with it.'

Simpson drank. It was the most wonderful wine he had ever known, with a strange warm aftertaste that seemed to seep upwards and flood his olfactory centres. He sighed deeply. 'Superb,' he said at last.

'Come on, come on, we want more than that; you got to do better than that. Give us a spot of imagery, kind of style, a reference to art, that kind of stuff.'

'It's – I don't know – it's the richness of summer, all the glory of ... of love and lyric poetry, a whole way of life, profound and ... some great procession of –'

'Ah, you turn me up,' the man said violently. 'This is a 2003 Château La Bouygue, reconstituted pre-phylloxera of course. Now, light and free, not rich in association but perfectly assured without any insincerity, instrumental where the 'Ols are symphonic, the gentleness of a Braque rather than the bravura of a Matisse. That's as far as you can go with it.'

•

Those who fancy substances less intoxicating than wine may consider a nice cup of cocoa, particularly at bedtime, a more suitable beverage. But cocoa, too, is supposed to have stimulating properties. Some years ago there was a story that it acted as an aphrodisiac. With that in mind, Arthur Marshall, a regular columnist on the *New Statesman* at the time, set his readers a competition. Entrants were required to write a poem on the subject of cocoa as an aphrodisiac. The best entry was submitted by Stanley J. Sharpless, winner of many another *New Statesman* prize.

I treasure the memory of Arthur Marshall reading the poem on Radio 4. The last line especially he seems to have made his own. It belongs to his voice just as 'A handbag!' belongs to Dame Edith Evans. Stanley J. Sharpless's poem is called 'Cupid's Nightcap'.

Half past nine – high time for supper;
'Cocoa, love?'; 'Of course, my dear.'
Helen thinks it quite delicious,
John prefers it now to beer.
Knocking back the sepia potion,
Hubby winks, says, 'Who's for bed?'
'Shan't be long,' says Helen softly,
Cheeks a-faintly flushing red.
For they've stumbled on the secret
Of a love that never wanes,
Rapt beneath the tumbled bedclothes,
Cocoa coursing through their veins.

•

It is not cocoa that stirs the clammy libido of a toad, nor yet a bit of pond weed or a passing fly.

You might imagine that I learned about the sex life of the toad from one of our nature programmes – but no: it was from our then Religious Affairs Correspondent, Gerald Priestland, that I gleaned these facts, during the course of *Yours Faithfully*, his weekly newsletter on Radio 4.

The story appeared first of all in *The Times*, submitted by Dr L. Fairchild, a zoologist of Duke University in North Carolina. Libby Purves read it and passed it on to Gerald Priestland. This is what he made of it.

The female toad, unaware of spiritual values, likes her mate big. But because she normally pairs in the dark, she has only one way of judging: the bigger the toad, the deeper his croak. However, there is a complicating factor, because a cold toad gives a deeper croak. Male toads therefore cunningly make for the coldest corner of the pond to deepen their croaks; and a female who thinks she is mating with a large, warm toad may in fact have been deceived by a small, cold one.

However, things do not stop there. Since all the toads are trying to chill off as much as possible, the large ones tend to win in the

end and take over the cold spot. Indeed, says Dr Fairchild, many of the smallest toads are forced right out of the pond and are obliged to sit on the bank, where (since it is warmer out of the water than in it, even in North Carolina) the small toads' croaking becomes even shriller and less enticing. However, there is still the chance consolation for the warm weaklings. For in order to get into the pond, the females do, of course, have to run the gauntlet of the bank – where, says Dr Fairchild, the small males make the most of their opportunities ... It should not be long before the large toads learn to lurk on the bank and shut up.

This week's problem is how to get a sermon out of all this, since surely it must mediate *something*. The Bible is not much help, since I find no reference to toads in it – only frogs. One might give the story the old analogy twist, and say, 'Dear friends, how very like toads we are, aren't we? Skirmishing to win the best place in the pond in the hope that our position will impress people, that the authority in our voice will win us a prize we do not strictly merit. And often we get away with it – because we are all of us croaking in the dark. Unlike the Supreme Being, who knows how small and insignificant we are, and who is not impressed by our hypocritical cries, we deceive each other and are in turn deceived. Some of us even drop out of the struggle that is set before us, and try to grab what we have not earned, even though it is more obvious than ever that we have not earned it. That is what the so-called permissive society is all about. When are we going to learn that the Creator has destined a proper voice and a proper place for each one of us? Yet all we, like toads, have gone astray ...'

●

But for every sinner there is always the possibility of repentance. In a sequence of two plays broadcast on Radio 3 called *Priest and Confessor*, the writer, Wally K. Daly, set the scene inside a confessional, as the priest and penitent prepare for the ancient ceremony of shriving.

The first play, a monologue, imagines what is going on inside the mind of the priest as he waits for the confessor to kneel at the other side of the grille in order to catalogue his sins and be absolved from them so that he may be in a state of grace for the Sabbath day.

Saturday night.

Have I got everything? A sandwich in case I get peckish halfway through. Book in case it gets intolerably boring.

Oh, it can get boring. It really can.

I mean, you'd think that people revealing their all would be a constant source of entertainment, wouldn't you.

Dark secrets of the soul spoken in whispers, but it can get surprisingly boring. Hence the book.

And this little torch.

Mind you, the amount of manipulation required to read without being twigged by the confessor is such that I do give rather severe penances if I have to resort to the book.

Actually I always give large penances for boring sins in any case.

As I see it, if they're going to force me to waste half of my favourite evening stifling yawns, they can pay the price with their knees.

The fastest you can say a whole rosary is about five minutes, even if you smash away at it. I think the record's about four minutes twenty-five seconds.

So I punish them pro rata.

Ten minutes, boredom, two rosaries.

Fifteen minutes, boredom, three. Get the idea? Very just.

Anyway, there's always the hope that big penances will drive them into going to Father O'Haggon the next week.

Vote with their feet, as it were.

Drive them across the nave, that's the answer.

Let him have the boring ones – I don't care.

Leave me room for more 'juicies'.

Now the children are different.

The sins of the children are small but never boring.

They bring a freshness and vitality to them. An air of adventure in their voices as they confess.

An amazement at their own discovery.

Dipping their toes carefully into the sea of sin, testing the texture of it. Feeling their way gently until puberty, when they can take the final plunge.

And then it's all worthwhile.

Their voices full of a strange mixture of pride and remorse.

The first time they confess – 'Forgive me, Father, but I had a bit last night.'

The number of times I've been tempted to say, 'Well done! You've finally made it.'

Ah. It's fascinating watching their sins mature.

You know. At times I've been tempted to write a sort of *Dr Spock of Sin*.

I'm sure there'd be a market for it.

Judge the intellect of your child by the level of sinning.

Is your child backward and only saying damn, when he should have reached bloody.

See what I mean?

●

A higher institute of learning was invented by Malcolm Bradbury and Christopher Bigsby for their Radio 3 comedy series *Patterson*. Patterson had recently joined the English faculty of an imaginary university and shortly afterwards he left his wife and children. Head of the English Department is the aptly named Professor Misty. He has asked his new junior colleague to deliver a lecture on his behalf, though what it is to be about is rather uncertain. The name Lawrence had been mentioned but was it D.H. or T.E.? In the midst of his domestic crisis, Patterson fights his way to Professor Misty's office and demands that the secretary should let him in.

Patterson: Mary, I've got to see Professor Misty.

Mary: That's funny, he's been looking all over for you. I think you'd better go straight in.

(*Tapping on door.*)

Misty: Ent-ter. Oh, Patterson, hard man to find. Look, I think I've found a young lady for you.

Patterson: Oh, yes?

Misty: Yes, I want you to meet Miss Oh Ah ...

Patterson: From China?

Misty: No, er, from ...

Valerie: Valerie Candle. From the United States.

Misty: That's it, Miss Candle from the States. This is Dr Patterson, about whom, Patterson, I called you in, or, rather, tried earlier to call you in, though you were not to be found, because, if I remember rightly, you've dundun.

Patterson: Oh, have I?

Misty: I thought you'd dundun. What did you do if it wasn't dun?

Patterson: Dundun?

Misty: Yes. Dunjundun. For your doctorate.

Patterson: Oh yes, how these things slip. I did write on John Donne for my PhD, yes.

Misty: I thought my memory wasn't amiss. Ah Miss, Oh Ah, the young lady, wants to do dun for hers too. Patterson, you don't think dun's been overdun, do you? There has been an awful lot dun.

Patterson: It depends on the topic.

Misty: Yes, well, I was suggesting to Miss Oh Ah that she might like to pick flowers.

Patterson: She might. But I'm sure we *could* find her a topic.

Misty: Yes, a topic. Pick the flower imagery of Donne.

Valerie: Actually I wanted to work on sex in Donne. His attitude to women.

Misty: I've been saying I thought Higher Degrees Committee in general probably greatly prefer flowers to sex.

Patterson: Perhaps Miss Candle and I should discuss it in more detail.

Misty: So you'd be willing to have the young lady under you? I was just trying to think. You have supervised before, haven't you? What happened to that black one I sent you?

Patterson: Oh, she left. Ran away, actually. She decided she'd rather go in for terrorism.

Misty: What about you, Miss Oh Ah?

Valerie: No, I'd rather write a thesis.

Misty: Well, then. If you're willing to take her on, Patterson? Of course, supervising a thesis requires great labour. Reading the stuff and scribbling on it. Still, it's an opportunity.

Patterson: Yes, I'll take her. Speaking of opportunities, Professor Misty, this lecture at twelve on Lawrence.

Misty: Oh yes, glad you could fill the breach.

Patterson: I just wondered. Which Lawrence is it?

Misty: Which Lawrence? Durrell. Lawrence Durrell.

Patterson: Oh.

Misty: I usually reminisce about Alexandria. Been there?

Patterson: No.

Misty: Tell them about something else then. Good, that's dun. Oh, Patterson, one more thing before you go. Mrs Misty and I would be delighted if you and your good wife could join us for dinner tonight. Someone's let us down at the last minute.

Patterson: My good wife?

Misty: You seem to be the only young man here these days who's still got one. I'm afraid this place is a veritable Goodwin Sands of marriage. Can't understand it. I'm afraid young people don't enjoy bondage any more.

Valerie: Oh, I don't know, Professor Misty.

Misty: My wife and I have always enjoyed being tied to the marriage bed. The tighter the better. Of course, I think it helps that we annotate together.

Valerie: Do what?

Misty: Go into the study and annotate together. Seven thirty for eight, then, Patterson?

Patterson: Yes, fine.

Misty: Oh, I do beg your pardon, Miss Oh Ah, I'm afraid I must seem dreadfully. Perhaps you'd grace our table too. It's always a pleasure to have a young woman. It's been some time ...

Valerie: Well, thank you, Professor, that's very gracious. I'd be delighted. And I could take the chance to talk properly with Dr Patterson.

Misty: Nothing very formal. Just a suit. I'd better get off to the faculty meeting. Patterson, must be time for your lecture. Do your best, push the *Quartet*, for some reason they've got a hundred copies in the bookshop. We'll be discussing you in Promotions Committee on Friday.

Patterson: Yes. Well. I'll see you this evening, Miss Candle.

●

Adultery can be made to sound light-hearted and amusing but, quite apart from the moral considerations, one consequence of it is that someone somewhere along the line gets hurt. The conventional view is that it is the one who is sinned against who suffers, but that may not always be the case.

On one of the Radio 4 *Time for Verse* series, Jeni Couzyn concentrated on the work of women poets. From her selection I have chosen a piece by the twentieth-century American writer Anne Sexton.

So much love poetry has been written by men who have woven fine verses about their coy or cruel mistresses that it comes as something of a shock to find a poem written from the mistress's point of view. It is called 'For My Lover, Returning Home to His Wife' and in it the deserted mistress is looking in on the wife her lover returns to.

She is all there.
She was melted carefully down for you
and cast up from your childhood,
cast up from your one hundred favorite aggies.

She has always been there, my darling.
She is, in fact, exquisite.
Fireworks in the dull middle of February
and as real as a cast-iron pot.

Let's face it, I have been momentary.
A luxury. A bright red sloop in the harbor.
My hair rising like smoke from the car window.
Littleneck clams out of season.

She is more than that. She is your have to have,
has grown you your practical your tropical growth.
This is not an experiment. She is all harmony.
She sees to oars and oarlocks for the dinghy,

has placed wild flowers at the window at breakfast,
sat by the potter's wheel at midday,
set forth three children under the moon,
three cherubs drawn by Michelangelo,

done this with her legs spread out
in the terrible months in the chapel.
If you glance up, the children are there
like delicate balloons resting on the ceiling.

She has also carried each one down the hall
after supper, their heads privately bent,
two legs protesting, person to person,
her face flushed with a song and their little sleep.

I give you back your heart.
I give you permission —

for the fuse inside her, throbbing
angrily in the dirt, for the bitch in her
and the burying of her wound —
for the burying of her small red wound alive —

for the pale flickering flare under her ribs
for the drunken sailor who waits in her left pulse,

for the mother's knee, for the stockings,
for the garter belt, for the call —

the curious call
when you will burrow in arms and breasts
and tug at the orange ribbon in her hair
and answer the call, the curious call.

She is so naked and singular.
She is the sum of yourself and your dream.
Climb her like a monument, step after step.
She is solid.

As for me, I am a watercolor.
I wash off.

●

The years from 1901 to 1905 were, apparently, rich in invention. During
that period 140,000 British patents were granted for things we have had to
learn to do without now, such as Jephson's Coffin for Indicating the Burial
Alive of a Person in a Trance, or Philip's Improved Animal Trap, which
caught mice without killing them.

In a programme on Radio 3 called *What Happened to Blattner's Self-
Acting Egg-Lifter?* compiled by Howard Goorney, the Edwardians were
revealed as an inventive generation.

Reader: Reading's New or Improved Adjustable Dress Holder and
Elevator provides a means by which a lady may adjust her dress or
skirt to any desired height immediately, in which position the dress
will be held by the holder until lowered or released as desired. The
suspender has a clamp at one end, held up by a chain which acts as a
metering device to regulate the amount of clothing revealed.

Narrator: Shorter skirts have put paid to these devices. And we
no longer regard ornamental moustaches as being the hallmark of
the gentleman:

Reader: Stephen's Improved Moustache Trainer guides the ends
of the moustache so that they assume and maintain certain
desired positions or directions in order to conform to a particular
fashion or fancy of the wearer.

Narrator: Modern washbasins with plug and outlet have
obviated the need for Dean and Farrar's Improved Soap Tablet or
Block.

Reader: This has as its primary object to effect economy. For this purpose the soap has moulded into it means for attachment to a tap, band or chain wound on a drum connected with a spring of sufficient strength to wind the tape on the drum when the soap is released by the user and so raise it out of the washbasin into a dry position but in convenient reach for use.

Narrator: Machines such as Hulsmeyer's Improved Hertzian Wave Protecting and Receiving Apparatus to Give Warning of the Presence of Metallic Bodies have probably been superseded by the advances of technology. If we eliminate all these and also Circus Manager Wulff's Improved Apparatus for Throwing Animals in the Air for Exhibition Purposes, we are still left with a fair number of simple, homely ideas intended to make day-to-day life easier for the Edwardians, and which could well cater for present-day needs. What happened to them? This could be very useful, for instance:

Reader: Leder's Foul Breath Indicator is a toilet article to enable persons to test their breath, and comprises an appliance in the shape of a curved tube made of any non-absorbent material. By breathing from the mouth through the tube any foulness or unpleasant state of the breath may be readily detected by the sense of smell.

Of course, one of the main preoccupations of inventors nowadays is how to solve the energy crisis. The comic writer Barry Pilton traced some new research into alternative sources of energy, which he published in his Radio 3 series *In a Nutshell*.

He told of a much underpublicized Nobel Prize ceremony where a certain Professor Heinz J. Soderstrom, well known for having developed miniaturized windmills for use inside the home, was honoured for proving conclusively that Europe's energy needs can be met by a grid system of power stations run on converted, medium-grade horse manure.

Obviously there will be difficulties. Capital investment in shovels will need to be drastically improved. But the scientific breakthrough has come in showing that Einstein's equation of $E=mc^2$ is only half the ballgame. For Soderstrom has proved that E (being energy) also equals the square root of 'hm', 'h' being horse and 'm' being manure. Or, to give it its scientific term, equine ordure.

As with all revolutionary concepts, there is opposition, people who pooh-pooh the idea. Already, vested financial interests are working on a coordinated attack. The oil companies are to publish a study claiming it would take eight horses per square foot to produce the required tonnage. Arthur Scargill says the plan is a political attack on the jobs of his members, and that he has proof that the professor is not only funded by the CBI, but that the government intends to use non-union animals. And in any case, he adds, coal-miner manure could supply at least four power stations. A spokesman for the gas industry pointed out that the cost would be far too cheap to make financial sense for businessmen. The nuclear-energy industry, while also disputing Professor Soderstrom's statistics, which they intend to look at some time next month, point out that, unlike plutonium, horse manure by-products have still not proved capable of producing any really effective bomb.

But Professor Soderstrom is undeterred. A quiet, unassuming man, the sort of Nobel scientist you wouldn't look at twice in the street, he has eyes which gleam with the reassuring knowledge that he alone has the answer to the world's problems. He is fond of quoting the famous Swedish witticism 'Science should be the handmaiden of progress, not the harlot of power' – a quotation from which he draws great succour and which he intends one day

64

to publish in six languages. In his brief acceptance speech, he outlined three essential advantages of his life-enhancing discovery. He pointed out that accessibility of the new fuel was a key factor, for – compared, say, with oil – less than 10 per cent of all known horse manure is in the North Sea. Also it is the only really mobile fuel, thereby cutting transport costs. In addition, he added, he could see no major technical problems, provided the horses could be persuaded of the urgency of the situation. And he finished his oration by paying particularly fulsome tribute to the Chinese who, with their usual long-sightedness, were responsible for inventing the product in the fifth century, by crossing a horse with food – during the Dung dynasty.

●

Close followers of my programme will know – and I hope not mind too much – that I enjoy poetry. When I was a girl there was one poem that I felt was particularly my own. It was called 'Middlesex', which is the county I grew up in and is now no more, and was written by John Betjeman. Like so many of his verses, it laments the passing of a lost Elysium, in this case the rural Middlesex he remembered. Again, as so often, the central figure in the poem is a girl. No hearty Miss Joan Hunter Dunn this one. She belongs strictly to the 'mushroomy, pine woody, evergreen smells' of Surrey. 'Fair Elaine' was from the commuter belt, a 'bobby soxer, fresh complexioned with Innoxa':

> Well-cut Windsmoor flapping lightly,
>   Jacqmar scarf of mauve and green
> Hiding hair which, Friday nightly,
>   Delicately drowns in Drene.

That early acquaintance with his work made me a lifelong fan of Betjeman. He seemed so often to touch the core of the ordinary things I knew about.

In later years he became more distinguished – the Poet Laureate and a knight. Thanks to television, and particularly to the producer Jonathan Stedall, we saw a lot of him on our television screens.

The BBC2 series *Time with Betjeman* showed us the Laureate at home in his elegant Chelsea house, chatting to friends. In one programme he was visited by Barry Humphries, whom he had met in Australia some years before, but, alas, they were interrupted by a gatecrasher – none other than the Australian Attaché for Cultural Affairs, Sir Les Patterson. He barged in, uninvited, complete with soup-stained tie and king-sized hip flask.

Les Patterson: Oh, excuse I. How are you, Sir John? Les Patterson. Barry – I'm not interrupting – you're not in the middle of a stanza or nothing like that?

John Betjeman: Oh no.

Les Patterson: I wouldn't want to get in the way of the muse. Very nice little compact little place too. *(Looking around room)* Worth a few shillings on the market at the moment.

John Betjeman: Oh, I don't think so.

Les Patterson: Oh, you bet. Settle myself down here if I may. Well, this is a – this, Sir Betjeman, is very much in the nature of a pilgrimage for me.

John Betjeman: I'm very glad to hear that.

Les Patterson: I've come all the way from Australia to this book-lined study. Where are we in London at the moment?

John Betjeman: In Chelsea, SW3. It's meant to be a rather Bohemian part, or it was.

Les Patterson: I bet you see the odd mini skirt going past the window? *(Wink and dirty chuckle.)*

John Betjeman: I suppose, yes. And a good many primrose front doors.

Les Patterson: Oh, the painting on the front doors. That's an Australian idea that's caught on over here.

John Betjeman: Oh yes.

Les Patterson: Painting the doors different colours. We've made a lot of contributions really to the cultural scene in the UK. I have to thank our friend, um Brian, sorry, Barry, er, Humphries – for effecting this introduction because I've wanted to get together with you to talk about a few cultural matters for a long time. I

66

wonder if you wouldn't mind if I just – um – just – *(Gets out whisky flask and pours some into teacup.)*

John Betjeman: No, not at all.

Les Patterson: Would you care for a drop yourself?

John Betjeman: I don't think so, thanks awfully. It's a bit early.

Les Patterson: Well, it is early, I must admit. We have a different timescale in Australia and they're open in Melbourne.

John Betjeman: Oh yes, are they, yes.

Les Patterson: According to my digital watch. It's a bit awe-inspiring for me, you understand – to be where it's at culture-wise in the UK.

John Betjeman: Yes.

Les Patter⋯⋯⋯ ⋯⋯rry there dressed up rather smartly. As a matter ⋯⋯⋯⋯⋯⋯⋯ ⋯⋯ suit for this occasion.

John Be⋯

Les P⋯ ⋯⋯⋯⋯⋯⋯⋯⋯⋯ ustralian craftsmanship, ⋯ ⋯⋯⋯⋯⋯⋯⋯ this little bloke. You send ⋯⋯⋯⋯⋯⋯⋯ he'll run you up – he does ⋯⋯⋯⋯⋯⋯⋯ and fawn.

Jo⋯

L⋯ ⋯⋯⋯⋯⋯⋯ ⋯our. Very popular in my ⋯ ⋯⋯⋯⋯⋯⋯ f course; there's a few little ⋯⋯⋯⋯⋯⋯ ⋯ry well and very good for entertain⋯⋯⋯ ⋯⋯⋯⋯ round at a lot of these books that you've got h⋯⋯ ⋯⋯⋯⋯. Have you read all of these volumes?

John Betjeman: Oh no, no. I have a lot of them for their beauty. I've read some of them, but not all.

Les Patterson: I'm a bit relieved to hear that because I think you and me in public life, we don't get too much time to dip into the odd volume ... They're deductible. Yes, books are deductible. My accountant – I was jogging with him this morning – my tax adviser, he said to me: buy books, they're deductible.

John Betjeman: Yes, yes, that's a nice idea.

Les Patterson: It's a tip. I hand it to you on a plate. My wife, Gwen, that is Lady Patterson, but Gwen to you, and I are very big fans. I think the first poem of yours, if I may say so, sir, was the one 'I must go down to the sea again, where the wind's like a whetted knife', and the 'Queen Kareen of Nivea'. 'Queen Kareen of Nivea –' The words escape me for the moment but beautiful.

John Betjeman: Oh yes, I'm so glad you think so. He's very good, isn't he? The man who wrote that?

•

It's strange to think of Sir John, the archetypal English old dodderer, visiting Australia and getting acquainted with marsupials, not to mention Barry Humphries. Even stranger, perhaps, that P. G. Wodehouse, who created the stock figure of the English silly ass, should end up in America writing lyrics for Broadway musicals.

The centenary of Wodehouse's birth was celebrated on Radio 4 in 1981 with a dip into his English vein. Michael Bakewell dramatized his book *Leave It to Psmith* (the P is silent, as in psittacosis).

P. G. Wodehouse: This, just in case any of you have been misled by the title, is one of the Blandings stories ... Blandings – a kind of earthly paradise. It's quite close to where my parents used to live in Shropshire, and the Blandings chronicles have multiplied like rabbits down the years since I first hit on the idea in a moment of desperation in 1915. In my childhood I had met with earls and butlers and younger sons in some profusion, and it struck me that the slick magazines would like to read about them. They did.

The saga you are going to hear tonight was written on Long Island in 1922 in a place revelling in the name of Great Neck. It is unique in the chronicles of Blandings in that it contains neither Lord Emsworth's captive balloon of a pig, the Empress, nor his irrepressible brother, Galahad, but it does contain Psmith.

68

Psmith (as if on the telephone): No, no, no – with a P. P-S-M-I-T-H. I should explain to you that I started life without the initial letter, and my father always clung ruggedly to the plain Smith. But it seemed to me that there were so many Smiths in the world that a little variety might be introduced. The P, I should add for your guidance, is silent, as in phthisis, psychic and ptarmigan. You follow me?

P. G. Wodehouse: Quite, as Lord Emsworth might have put it, and it is to his lordship that we must now turn. Clarence, Ninth Earl of Emsworth, whose manner I have frequently compared to a wet sock, is in a melancholy condition. He looks blearily out over his beautiful gardens, but his heart does not rejoice.

Emsworth: Just a blur. Can't make out a thing.

P. G. Wodehouse: For he has lost his glasses and, without them, is blind as a bat.

(Door opens, off.)

Emsworth (startled): Who's that?

Beach: It is I, your lordship, Beach.

Emsworth: Have you found them?

Beach: I have searched assiduously, your lordship, but without avail. Thomas and Charles also announce non-success. Stokes has not yet made his report.

Emsworth: Ah!

Beach: I am redispatching Thomas and Charles to your lordship's bedroom. I trust that their efforts will be rewarded.

(Door closes.)

Emsworth (mutters): Blind as a dratted bat.

(Door opens.)

Freddie: Hello guv'nor. Hear you've lost your glasses.

Emsworth: That is so.

Freddie: Nuisance, what?

Emsworth: Undeniably.

Freddie: Ought to have a spare pair.

Emsworth: I have broken my spare pair.

Freddie: Tough luck! And lost the other?

Emsworth: And, as you say, lost the other.

Freddie: Have you looked for the bally things?

Emsworth: I have.

Freddie: Must be somewhere, I mean.

Emsworth: Quite possibly.

Freddie: Where did you see them last?

Emsworth: Go away!

Freddie: Eh?

Emsworth: Go away!

Freddie: Go away?

Emsworth: Yes, go away!

Freddie: Right ho!

(Door closes.)

Emsworth (profound sigh, not untinged with vexation): Blind as a dratted bat.

P. G. Wodehouse: Earls, butlers and younger sons. See what I mean?

●

Let us now turn to the world of academe, where serious scholarship can be rewarded by a university professorship. Once you have achieved that status, life can be extremely rosy. That was the picture painted, at any rate, by David Lodge, Professor of English at Birmingham University, in a talk on Radio 3 in the series *The Living Novelist*.

Professor Lodge's own novel *Small World*, set in 1979, describes the academic jet set to which he himself belongs: the world of learned missions, international conferences convened to discuss serious matters such as literary criticism and literary theory, while also providing the profs with generous enough conference grants to sample the fleshpots at the usually exotic locations. This is how the fourth part of *Small World* begins.

WhheeeeeeeeeeeeEEEEEEEEEEEEEEEEE!

To some people, there is no noise on earth as exciting as the sound of three or four big fan-jet engines rising in pitch, as the plane they are sitting in swivels at the end of the runway and, straining against its brakes, prepares for takeoff.

Whheeeeeeee!

Europe, here we come! Or Asia, or America, or wherever. It's June, and the conference season is well and truly open. In Oxford and Rummidge, to be sure, the students still sit at their desks in the examination halls, like prisoners in the stocks, but their teachers are able to flit off for a few days before the semester of the academic year is already finished, papers have been graded, credits awarded, and the faculty are free to collect their travel grants and head east, or west, or wherever their fancy takes them.

Wheeeeeeee!

The whole academic world seems to be on the move. Half the passengers on transatlantic flights these days are university teachers. Their luggage is heavier than average, weighed down with books and papers – and bulkier, because their wardrobes must embrace both formal wear and leisurewear, clothes for attending lectures in, and clothes for going to the beach in, or to the Museum, or the Schloss, or the Duomo, or the Folk Village. For that's the attraction of the conference circuit; it's a way of converting work into play, combining professionalism with tourism, and all at someone else's expense.

Write a paper and see the world! I'm Jane Austen – fly me! Or Shakespeare, or T. S. Eliot, or Hazlitt. All tickets to ride, to ride the jumbo jets. Wheeeeeeeeeeee!

The air is thick with the babble of these wandering scholars' voices, their questions, complaints, advice, anecdotes. Which airline did you fly? How many stars does the hotel have? Why isn't the conference hall air-conditioned? Don't eat the salad here, they use human manure on the lettuce. Laker is cheap, but their terminal at LA is the pits. Cathay Pacific gives you free drinks in economy. Qantas has the best safety record among the international airlines, and Columbia the worst – one flight in three never arrives at its destination (OK a slight exaggeration). On every El Al flight there are three secret servicemen with guns concealed in their briefcases, trained to shoot hijackers on sight – when taking something from your inside pocket, do it slowly and smile. Did you hear about the Irishman who tried to hijack a plane to Dublin! It was already going there. Wheeeeeeeeeeeeee!

●

Not all plane journeys are so jolly. On 19 April 1979 a Boeing 727 with eighty-nine people on board went out of control and came plummeting out of the sky. It fell 33,000 feet in 44 seconds yet somehow just missed crashing.

The disaster was re-created for BBC1 by Bill Curtis, correspondent of the American station CBS. The remarkable thing was that he did not use actors but actually brought together the original passengers and crew to relive the most terrifying moment of their lives.

At first, all was going smoothly. The passengers settled down for the flight, one lady went to the toilets at the back, a man moved away from his wife to be in a smoking area and the pilot, Captain Gibson, requested clearance to ascend to 39,000 feet. His fellow crew members did speed checks and made final adjustments to the power.

Captain Gibson: The first thing I noticed was a very slight vibration. You could feel it in the balls of your feet, you know, just a high-frequency vibration in the airplane.

Man (passenger): All of a sudden, there was sort of a shudder, where the whole plane shook.

Mary Butera: What is that?

(Clatter of falling dishes.)

Girl (passenger): Ma, what's happening?

Mother (passenger): I don't know.

Girl (screaming): The checkers fell, Mom.

Mother: Don't worry about the checkers.

Woman (passenger): We're going to die, and it's going to fall.

Captain Gibson: The nose went down, and I couldn't control the roll right. Get 'em up!

Banks: I looked towards Hoot.

72

Captain Gibson: Get 'em up! Get 'em up! Get 'em up!

Banks: He's hollering, 'Get 'em up!' – only no one's responding yet.

Captain Gibson: Get 'em up. We're going over.

Kennedy: And he was telling me to pull the spoiler handle. He let go of the wheel with his hand and reached over and pulled them up himself.

Banks: And that doesn't even slow the plane down. That doesn't even start to slow the plane down.

Kennedy: The airplane was flying itself. It was doing its own thing. And then we just tailed off the nearest thing and just went into a big spiral.

Man (passenger): It felt just as if a giant hand were propelling us at an extreme rate of acceleration.

Man (passenger): One of the stewardesses was going flying by. So, I grabbed her.

Man (passenger): And the screaming of these engines were just horrifying.

Woman (passenger): The sound was like a rushing, screaming sound, like those old movies when a plane is hit.

Man (passenger): We held on for dear life.

Woman (passenger): Everything did go into slow motion.

Man (passenger): Pushed back into the seat, deeper and deeper and deeper into the seat. You thought that you were gonna run out of cushion.

Holly Wicker: My attention at that point was totally focused on a five-pound baby on my lap, who was turning blue. All I could think was that I had to give her mouth-to-mouth.

Woman (passenger): And I just figured that, if anybody had a chance, it would be in the back. There'd be nothing left of us in the front.

Mrs Merrill: All I knew is I had to get out of there, as though getting out of the bathroom was going to make everything okay.

Man (passenger): I found myself yelling, at the top of my voice, instructions to the pilot.

Woman (passenger): I was able to move my hand up and touch my face, and it felt like stone. Maybe this is the way you feel when you're dead.

Mrs Merrill: I felt like something was coming down on top of me, like the old horror movies – big cement block is coming down on the heroine and is going to crush her to death.

Flight Attendant: Our plane is descending at the rate of 76,000 feet a minute.

Captain Gibson: Scott was on the – on the control wheel with me; tried going forward, backward, reversing the controls; ran the spoiler handle up and down at least a couple of times. Nothing was effective at all. It'd be like sitting in your car on a grease rack or something, where nothing's hooked up.

Kennedy: Yeah, I just knew that what we were doing wasn't regaining control of the aircraft.

Banks: And I literally say to myself, 'My God, it's all over. I wonder what it's going to feel like to hit.'

Captain Gibson: I think we just accepted the fact that everybody was going to die.

Man (passenger): So, I asked the Lord if he wouldn't save all the passengers in the plane, perform one miracle.

Man (passenger): All human beings have an end. This is mine. And I found myself ready for it.

Man (passenger): I won't feel any pain; it'll just be lights going out.

Woman (passenger): I knew I was going to die alone.

Man (passenger): And I said, 'I love you, Lord.'

Woman (passenger): Please make it fast.

Man (passenger): I shut my eyes and expected to hit the ground.

●

Miraculously they did not hit the ground. The plane somehow managed to pull upwards out of that terrible nose dive, leaving the passengers scattered and shocked but alive to tell the tale.

Fortunately not many of us have to face death in such extreme conditions but it is, nonetheless, something we will have to face one day. For some people the worst part of it is thinking about what will happen to those they have left behind and the grief that will be caused.

The actor John le Mesurier died recently, and as part of an obituary tribute to him Radio 4's *P.M.* programme played some words about death that he himself had recorded. They were written by an American Indian and though they are sad they have an element of cheer in them which exactly accords with John le Mesurier's wish to have his own demise described as having 'conked out'.

When I am dead
Cry for me a little
Think of me sometimes
But not too much.
Think of me now and again
As I was in life
At some moments it's pleasant to recall
But not for long.
Leave me in peace
And I shall leave you in peace
And while you live
Let your thoughts be with the living.

●

Anthony Nolan died when he was not quite eight years old. In his short life his name became well known – as it still is today – because of the battle his mother, Shirley Nolan, fought to have a bone-tissue-matching laboratory set up so that children like him could be helped to survive bone-marrow disease.

The Anthony Nolan Foundation, which continues the work in his name, can now provide a child anywhere in the world with a donor for a transplant and a chance to live. Anthony Nolan himself was not so lucky.

Shirley Nolan spoke vividly about her struggle for her son's life on the BBC2 series *The Light of Experience*. More recently, in a new series called *The Light of Experience Revisited*, Bel Mooney invited people who had told their stories some years ago to return to the studio and discuss how they have coped with life since then. Shirley Nolan was the first to return and Bel Mooney asked her if her son's death had allowed her a complexity of feeling about him that she had not had when he was alive.

Shirley Nolan: No, I certainly believed, until six weeks before Anthony's death, that he would survive. I always had this tremendous feeling that somehow we were going to win through and that was my biggest ... my biggest disappointment, I think, in my entire life: to come to terms with looking at my son and saying to myself, 'He is going to die,' and we looked at each other. He knew he was going to die. He transmitted his feelings to me. I knew he was going to die.

Bel Mooney: You seem to be implying that you yourself lost the will for him to live, that you cut off the willpower.

Shirley Nolan: No. It was something that ... It was a medical decision. I had fought for Anthony as long as the end ... the survival was going to be that Anthony could lead a normal healthy life: and fortunately, despite his initial brain haemorrhage, his suffering, his hair loss, his ... the tragedy of his suffering during that seven years, he was, incredibly, this bouncy, smiling, courageous little chap. He never, never whimpered, and it was this – it was a sort of symbiotic thing. We ... we felt we were fighting together. But when it came to the point that transfusions could no longer be given in his arms ... He was having transfusions through his ankles, was having transfusions through his neck, but I flatly refused when it came to transfusing him through his head, and it was a point of me accepting the fact that we had lost, that nothing further, medically, could be done.

Bel Mooney: But after he died, did you feel guilty because you'd accepted that?

Shirley Nolan: There's two emotions now that I feel that obviously I didn't feel then, because Anthony was alive, this tremendous guilt that all parents feel. I've spoken to other parents who have lost children, either with bone-marrow deficiency, a child that was stillborn, a child that was born handicapped, a child who was involved in a road accident, a child who was murdered. The parents always feel that they are to blame.

Bel Mooney: Do you think also that he suffered unnecessarily from being kept alive so long?

Shirley Nolan: No. Anthony wanted to live. Of that I'm sure. My guilt lies in the knowledge that at times I gave in. In my book I actually said, at one point, when Mother had to go to Australia, when her only other grandson was killed in a road accident – I was trying to cope with Anthony on my own, which was virtually impossible, and I'd reached the stage where he was flinging his cup of drinks up the wall and ... and totally uncontrollable, and I grabbed him and shook him and said, 'Die, damn it! If you're going to die, die. Get on with it.' And that intensity, this sort of love/hate relationship that a parent has with a sick child or a handicapped child, the emotions are so turbulent, so fierce, so demanding, that either they destroy ... they destroy you or they motivate you to great heights, and I think Anthony motivated me to be a better person. I took my example from him. I ... I wasn't keeping Anthony alive. Anthony was keeping Anthony alive.

●

Maya Angelou is the bestselling female black writer in the world. Her roots are in the American South, an area she describes graphically in her autobiography.

The first volume of her autobiography, *I Know Why the Caged Bird Sings*, was reviewed on BBC2's *Bookmark* programme. Readings from it and interviews with the author and others helped to form a picture of the life of this quite extraordinary woman.

She started out her working life as the first black conductorette on the San Francisco trams. She was also a prostitute and a night-club singer; she toured the world in *Porgy and Bess* and she appeared in the film *Roots*. The child of divorced parents, she was sent to the Deep South with her brother to be brought up by her grandmother in the small town of Stamps, Arkansas, at a time when black and white people did not mix.

Maya Angelou (reading): Crossing the black area of Stamps which in childhood's narrow measure seemed a whole world, we were obliged by custom to stop and speak to every person we met, and Bailey felt constrained to spend a few minutes playing with each friend. There was a joy in going to town ... But the pleasure fled when we reached the white part of town ... We were explorers walking without weapons into man-eating animals' territory.

In Stamps the segregation was so complete that most black children didn't really, absolutely, know what whites looked like. Other than that they were different, to be dreaded, and in that dread was included the hostility of the powerless against the powerful, the poor against the rich, the worker against the worked for and the ragged against the well dressed ...

Whitefolks couldn't be people because their feet were too small, their skin too white and see-throughy, and they didn't walk on the balls of their feet the way people did – they walked on their heels like horses.

People were those who lived on my side of town. I didn't like them all, or, in fact, any of them very much, but they were people. These others, the strange pale creatures that lived in their alien unlife, weren't considered folks. They were whitefolks.

Narrator: At the heart of Maya Angelou's first book lies the account of her rape as a small child. For five years afterwards she'd speak to no one except her elder brother, Bailey, and even writing about it years later did nothing to exorcize the nightmare.

Maya Angelou: It so happened that I am the most read black female writer in the world. It has so happened that I direct movies in Hollywood, I compose scores for movies and I'm the Reynolds Professor at Wake Forest University, a very rich white Southern school. And I have the chair. I'm healthy and reasonably attractive to the men who I choose to be attractive to, and not once from the time when I was seven and a half until this moment, not one day has passed that I have not thought about the rape. Not one day.

Herbert Mitgang (of the New York Times*):* There's one scene that is both universal and frightening, even reading it many years after it happened. The frustration leaps off the printed page for me – and that's when her grandmother, who she called Momma, comes to take her to the dentist – and there's only one white dentist in town – and this poor child is in pain – and the dentist – she's begging, and ironically the dentist's name is Lincoln – and he says, 'Annie,' the dentist says, 'Annie, you know I don't treat nigger coloured people.' 'I know dentists, Lincoln, but this here is just my little grandbaby and she ain't going to be no trouble to you.' And he goes on and says 'Everybody has a policy, Annie.

My policy is that I'd rather stick my hand in a dog's mouth than in a nigger's.'

•

While that may have been the reality of life in the South, over on the West Coast of the United States they were busy manufacturing the myth. Chief among the architects of the American dream world was Walt Disney, creator of Mickey Mouse, Donald Duck and a host of other lovable characters. However, Walt himself was not a lovable character, according to a Radio 3 documentary about him compiled by Russell Davies. Davies called his programme *Waltschmerz*, which is a pun on the German word *Weltschmerz*, meaning sorrow at the state of the world – and certainly the programme told something of the sad side of the Walt Disney success story.

Russell Davies talked to many of the animators who worked for Disney in the thirties and forties and from them he discovered that Disney was a hard taskmaster who paid great attention to detail, but apparently his own talents were somewhat limited. As one of his staff said, 'He had no knowledge of draughtsmanship, no knowledge of music, no knowledge of literature, no knowledge of anything really.' What he did have was great skill as an editor and a willingness to take risks by doing things with animation that had never been attempted before.

Russell Davies: Not for the first or last time, Disney had made a gambler's investment in a huge project. On the *Lux Hour* radio show of 20 December 1937, the day before the premiere of the picture, Cecil B. DeMille payed tribute to a production conceived on his own epic scale.

Cecil B. DeMille: Tomorrow night in the Carthay Circle Theater, scene of epic Hollywood premieres, another chapter in motion-picture history will be written when Walt Disney presents the first full-length, animated film ever made: *Snow White and the Seven Dwarfs*. For giving us Mickey Mouse, Donald Duck and the *Silly Symphonies*, the world owes Walt a great debt. He was the first to make animated cartoons in sound and then in colour. And with *Snow White* he pioneers once again in a picture that took three years to make and involved more than two million individual drawings.

Ollie Johnston: Everbody called it 'Walt's Folly'. All Hollywood was really laughing at him. But we went to the premiere of the thing over at the Carthay Circle and all these movie people were there – big stars – and they were all completely taken with it; they clapped at the right places and laughed, and spontaneous applause at the end; it was a thrilling time.

Russell Davies: These were the charming years of the Disney output when the drawings still show the artists' newborn delight in what bending, stretching, squashing and snapping bodies can be made to do. They have that ramshackle eccentricity that is part of the joy of discovery. But even in these happy times Disney's success was achieved at the cost of some heartache to individual animators, as Art Babbitt recalls.

Art Babbitt: In *Pinocchio* he threw away, oh, a tremendous amount of work, and it was beautifully animated, but it slowed up the story. And that took a lot of courage, because he didn't have that sort of money to throw away. This happened in *Snow White* too; there were several sequences that were thrown away that were beautifully done.

Russell Davies: Largely by Ward Kimball, who'd been allotted two lively scenes by Disney: the dwarfs' soup-drinking display, and their bed-building sequence.

Ward Kimball: He brought me up to his office and he was very sad – he tried to act that way – he said he thought the soup sequence was wonderful. And we were just halfway through the bed-building. But, he says, we've got to get on with the story and we're over the time and something's got to go. I said, 'Walt, maybe I'm not cut for this thing, I'm very discouraged and . . .' He never really heard me. He started talking about this great picture that they were going to be making, he was always thinking ahead; *Snow White* was in the can as far as he was concerned. *Pinocchio*! And he says, 'We're gonna have this little cricket character.' He says, 'We're adding that to the story because we have got to have something to bounce Pinocchio's gaining knowledge off of – it'll be his conscience, and you are just the man to handle this.' And I stood there and my eyes started blinking and he sold me! I walked out and I didn't quit; it was a damn good thing I didn't! Walt was a super salesman!

●

Over on the East Coast of the United States lies the city of New York. You either hate it or you love it. I go along with all those stickers: I love it. It is a city of independent spirits, of dry humour and, above all, it works. The logic of the layout of the streets on a grid-iron system means that you have to be pretty dumb to get lost. At least, that is how it was when I was last there, but things change fast in the city and with a high population density plus a building boom the whole place may grind to a halt and become the magnificent catastrophe that the architect le Corbusier called it long ago.

A Magnificent Catastrophe was the title Stephen Games gave to his documentary on New York for Radio 3. He talked to planners, architects and city dwellers about what it is like to live and work in such an overcrowded environment. He came upon an interesting observation from William H. Whyte which may overturn a few preconceived ideas about the inhuman nature of urban life. William H. Whyte is the author of *The Organization Man* and he has made a study of the workings of the street.

William H. Whyte: One of the first things that we noticed when we were doing our studies of street life, I was very interested to find out when two people run into each other, two friends, how far out of the pedestrian traffic stream they will move, and I hypothesized that they would move, you know, right next to a building – there is about a foot that people never use – and so we mounted time-lapse cameras, and what was interesting, as we mapped these things, we saw quite the contrary to what we expected. People didn't move out of the traffic stream, they moved into it; and the longer the conversation the more apt it is to be in the middle. You can see this on Fifth Avenue very clearly, particularly at lunchtime.

Whenever you see two people, you know, talking, watch where they are and I'll lay you money that more times than not they are right smack in the middle of a corner. Now if you ask those people what kind of a sitting place would they like, 'Oh I want quiet, a walled enclave, a lot of greenery, quiet, get away from the city.' They never go near such a place. Let me give you a good example: Green Acre Park, I don't know if you've seen it; it's a very small, little park. It's all of forty-two feet by a hundred feet and it's on 53rd Street and it's very simple and people will always tell you how quiet it is. Why do you go to Green Acre Park? 'Oh, I enjoy the quiet, I enjoy ... so uncrowded.' It is in fact the most crowded place of its kind in New York. It is quite noisy, the decibel count is quite high; on a nice summer day the place will be jammed with at least, say, about 180 to 185 people – it's a lot of

people for that small place yet they don't feel crowded, and it's wonderful to see how people can really enjoy a rather high density as long as they feel there's choice. So when I go to other cities and I don't see much of that, I feel a little proud, and the reason I don't see much of it in certain cities is simply there is not enough density of people. It's like a party – you need a certain number of people you know to make that thing work and this is the mark of a great city.

Stephen Games: Speculation about the mechanics of the city is nevertheless a long way from being a precise science. Richard Sennett, in his book *The Fall of Public Man*, has talked about the paradox of people being isolated by their own visibility in the dead public space of a modern city. William Whyte isn't convinced.

William H. Whyte: People love to talk about the anonymity of a great city. But I think you find more human contact and human interchange often in a very crowded place than you will in a much less one. Now we have a . . . as all great places have, we have quite a few street characters and one of the greatest contributions they make is what I call triangulation. Here's what I mean by that: they furnish a connection between people that otherwise doesn't exist. Okay, you and I, we're standing on a street corner, we've never ... never known each other from Adam. Mr Magoo is our traffic director, who's a wonderful character, and he's just a typical, what everyone thinks a New Yorker is like; he's got this rasping voice, very brusque, very rude and he's out there directing traffic: 'Hey, lady, where the hell do you think you're going!' And people are there and they're laughing and I turn to you and say, 'Do you know who that guy is?' and I'll say it in a tone of voice that you reserve for close friends, and I'll say, 'I saw him the other week', or 'I think he's a cop', or something like that. You will go away, but for one brief instant we talk. As you can see, I am hopelessly biased; I do think it happens other places but I know it happens here, I know it happens here.

●

One of the glories produced by our English countryside is the apple. Though many of our fine varieties have disappeared, you can still find a proper English russet, a Worcester pearmain, a Cox's Orange Pippin or a May Queen. Concern for the preservation of our apple varieties began to be voiced in the 1940s. In a programme called *In Praise of Older Apples*, Dr Joan Morgan quoted from a broadcast made by Morton Sand just after the war. He had called his talk *Apples – Going, Going, Gone*.

I started to collect disappearing and apparently doomed apples in 1941. At that time, some 50 per cent of my skeleton list of about fifty names could still be got in ones and twos from a few older firms scattered about the country. By 1942 the percentage had dropped to 35, and by 1943 it had dropped to well under 25. This year, the number of the old varieties still offered has fallen to less than 10 per cent of my list. Well, strings of names are dull things to have to listen to so I shall mention no more than five included in that list of mine, and these will have to be representative of only one region. The Wessex apple I shall single out rather invidiously won't be the charmingly named and subtly spiced Cornish Gilly Flower; it won't be its even older fellow countryman, the Pearless Cornish Aromatic – although I could be lyrical about both of them. It won't be either of those now extinct Somerset apples, the Pomeroy and Court of Wick, which I was never lucky enough to taste. Those who have tasted them speak of them reverently with shining eyes, drawing in their breath with a gasp of keenly remembered delight. No, my choice is that glorious Ashmeade's Kernel. It was raised by a Dr Ashmeade of Gloucester in about 1720, and I choose it because it was my father's favourite apple and he was no mean judge. He happened upon Ashmeade's Kernel quite by chance and without ever having heard of it after fifty years' unquestioning loyalty to Ribston, Blenheim and Cox, with occasional imperialistic interludes of those splendid Tasmanian Sturmer Pippins. It was his considered opinion that Ashmeade's Kernel was just perceptibly superior to any of those august four. What an apple; what suavity of aroma. Its initial Madeira-like mellowness of flavour overlies a deeper honeyed nuttiness; crisply sweet – not sugar sweet but the succulence of a well-devilled marrow bone. Surely no apple of greater distinction or more perfect balance can ever have been raised anywhere on earth.

●

In her researches into apples, Dr Morgan also came across the writings of Edward Bunyard, whose book *The Epicure's Companion* was published in 1929. Curiously, it was he who was responsible for introducing the Golden Delicious, that wretched woolly excuse for an apple that we now import in such numbers from France. I am sure he would have no truck with it these days – any more than he did with that Frenchified pudding, the tart.

Reader: All good things in England are enclosed: commons, gardens, remittances and pies – that's our humour. But the pie, the pie of all pies, the quintessence of piety, is the apple pie.

Joan Morgan: An opinion certainly shared by George IV's Foreign Secretary, Lord Dudley, who was said never to dine comfortably without apple pie, complaining audibly throughout the grandest dinners if he found it missing from the menu. Bunyard had plenty to say on apple pies. Not only on the variety of apple to use but also on the quality of the crust.

Reader: Shall it be short or long? Not too short, I think. The crust which crumbles into dust like a shortcake is too suggestive of our common end. Furthermore, it does not take up the flavour of the apple as it should. Nor again too long. A hard steely crust accepts no advantage from the apple and is altogether too assertive. No, it must be a collaborating crust, remembering always that it is but a performer in a duet. It must cover the pie, agreed, but it must also run a little down the side and touch the fruit with a gentle hand. Here you get the most intimate passages of your pie. And then the apples – and here I do not argue, I'm telling you – not every apple is worthy. The best English apples by long training know how to behave in a pie. They melt but do not squelch; they inform but do not predominate. An apple should preserve its individuality and form, not go to a pale mealy squash but become soft and golden. In flavour it must be sharp, or what's the use of your Barbados sugar? It should have some distinct flavour of its own. Fulfilling all the conditions comes Golden Noble – golden before and after cooking, transparent in the pie and in every way delectable. This is a September/October apple and after this we begin our Bramleys. At the end of the season comes Wellington, the fruit which has found a way to keep its acidity till June and has a crisp transparency quite ideal for pies.

●

BBC TV South produced a series about Dorsetmen. The first programme showed a new angle on one of the best known Dorsetmen of them all, Thomas Hardy. There are not many people alive today who remember Hardy personally. Harold Macmillan is one and Gertrude Bugler is another.

When Gertrude Bugler was seventeen she joined the Dorchester Amateur Dramatic Society known as the Hardy Players. It was during her time with that company that she became Hardy's first stage Tess in *Tess of the D'Urbervilles*.

Gertrude Bugler first met Thomas Hardy in 1913, when she was acting in a dramatization of *The Woodlanders* and he came along to a rehearsal. He was not, she told Dennis Skillicorn – despite what you might expect from much of the tone of his work – he was not at all glum.

Gertrude Bugler: There was Thomas Hardy, smiling, and he said, 'Well, Marty, how do you like your part?' I said, 'I like it very much.'

Dennis Skillicorn: Gertrude became a leading actress with the Hardy Players, starring in various roles in adaptations of the Wessex novels. But her best part came in 1924, when Hardy allowed the Players to stage the dramatization of *Tess of the D'Urbervilles*, and at Hardy's request Gertrude became the first ever Tess. The play was a great success, so much so that it was decided to put it on in London's West End with a professional cast, with one exception – Gertrude was to play Tess. Hardy was delighted.

Gertrude Bugler: He said he was pleased that Tess was going to London and that I should be the first person to create Tess, to play Tess in London. And then he said, 'If anyone asks you if you know Thomas Hardy, say, "Yes, he was my friend."'

Dennis Skillicorn: But her dreams of London were shattered when Florence, Hardy's second wife, called on her at home.

Gertrude Bugler: There was a knock on the door of the little cottage, here in Bedminster, and Mrs Hardy came in. There was a car outside. And she said her husband didn't know she had come, but she felt she must come. He was in such a nervous state. She felt that he would want to go to London if *Tess* was put on there. He was an old man, and it would be too much for him. His reputation would be gone. I mustn't go to London. And would I give up the idea because it would be very, very bad for him, bad for his reputation and so on. She went on a long way and I realized she was upset, very nervous, very agitated. I was bewildered. I couldn't understand, I didn't know what it was about. I didn't see why Thomas Hardy shouldn't go to see his own play in London. But she was asking me to do it – evidently, it was necessary or she wouldn't be so upset.

Dennis Skillicorn: Do you think Florence, then, was the jealous woman?

Gertrude Bugler: I'm pretty sure that she was.

●

As I mentioned, Harold Macmillan, now the Earl of Stockton, also remembers meeting Thomas Hardy. It was while working with the family publishing business, when he met many of the firm's authors, including Rudyard Kipling and Hugh Walpole. Talking to Ludovic Kennedy on the BBC1 programme *Reflections*, where he looked back over the events of his long life, Macmillan recalled his impressions of Thomas Hardy.

The impressive thing about him was his – and I think about his books, somebody asked me why they've lasted so long, because they aren't very well written really, the stories are good – I think it was the deep sincerity of the man. He never wrote a word or said a word he didn't believe to be true. And I think the extraordinary thing about *Tess* – although some of it is rather, and all his books, some of them are rather laboured – is their sincerity. That's why they've lasted. And he was like that. He was like a little countryman with red-apple cheeks – you know, the kind of countryman who's lived out of doors all the time and he has red cheeks with all the little lines like a pippin. He was like that. And then he was very amusing, and rather – not cynical but, I mean, he didn't like nonsense. There was a great story – it wasn't my story, it was my uncle's story; he went down to see him at Dorchester. And of course during most of his life, nobody, his books were not successful, and I don't think any of them had any success at all, so he stopped writing them really. He never wrote another book after *Jude the Obscure*, you know, because it was condemned as improper and that upset him very much. But he went down to see him, and by the end of his life Hardy was suddenly discovered, you know, and he became – you know what the English are – he became fashionable, and so the smart people went to see him and I think the second Mrs Hardy rather liked this, but he was amused by it. And my uncle had a wonderful story that he was there at lunch one day, and a lot of the smart people had come over, some from Wilton and some from great houses nearby, about twelve of them in a little room, and one of these rather, rather, you know, ladies said in rather a gushing way, 'Oh, Mr Hardy, tell us about Tess, what did she mean to you?' And Hardy called down the table and said, 'The duchess here is asking about Tess and says what did she mean to you. I said she's been a good milch cow to you and me, Fred, hasn't she?' That was very like him.

●

In the same programme, Lord Stockton spoke of his political career. In his early days as a Member of Parliament there were fewer committees than there are today and a new Member had to make his reputation on the floor of the House. Parliament was dominated by the House of Commons. It was there that you learned the difficult art of public speaking. Ludovic Kennedy asked Harold Macmillan who had taught him that art.

Well, I was very lucky. In the '24 Parliament, I was an earnest young man and I made a speech – the Depression was beginning, you know, and all that – which I think Maynard Keynes had helped me with. And it was quite a good speech for a young man. I mean, the matter was good. And by chance of course, when your speaker is young, there are perhaps fifty, a hundred people in the House – you're lucky if you get that. Even then, perhaps a hundred. It so happened that Lloyd George was sitting in the House and afterwards he came up to me – I didn't know him, because in the war, I was, he was – I didn't know him at all. He came up to me and said, 'Macmillan, you made a very good and interesting speech.' So I was rather pleased and said, 'Thank you very much, sir.' He said, 'But if you don't mind my telling you, you haven't got the faintest idea how to make a speech.' So I said, 'But will you show me, sir?' 'Yes,' he said, 'I will, if you'll come to my room.' And that's when I began a long friendship with him. 'But,' he said, 'first of all, your speech had about twenty points; it would have been a very good article in an economic journal. In a speech here you want one point, if you're a young man; two if you're a minister, perhaps, but even that's difficult; three if you're Prime Minister. You go round and round it, you say it this way and that way, you have the funny bits, and so on. Secondly, your speech was like a gramophone record of a sermon; you just went on and on and on on the same note. It doesn't really much matter what you say, to be quite frank, but what matters is how you say it. Now you must get up, always when you get up to make a speech in a – anywhere you are – say to yourself, "Vary the pitch and vary the pace." There must be the quick bit, the heavy bit; it's like a symphony, you know. And that is the great thing. And make, so that when you go back and somebody in the smoking room says, "That fellow made a good speech," the other person says, "What did he say?" – well, you said twenty things. What you want him to reply is: "He said there's no difference between black and white," or whatever the point was.' Well, he taught me everything.

●

If you ever have a hankering to follow in Lord Stockton's footsteps and one day become a Member of Parliament, maybe even Prime Minister, you might like to take advantage of Patrick Hannan's handy guide on *How to*

88

Be an MP. It was one of a series of *How to Be* ... programmes he did for Radio 4 earlier this year.

The job does not sound all that attractive. Salary £16,106 a year; no allowances, no job security, no union representation, no industrial tribunals. If, after that catalogue of discouragement, you still want to be an MP, consider this. If you are short of stature, join Labour. If you are tall, join the Conservatives. Think too which party you would be most comfortable in sartorially.

Patrick Hannan: Dark suits, unpressed of course, belong among the Conservatives, although there's been something of an outbreak of the Austin Reeds in the SDP. For Labour it's a jacket and trousers which *must not match.* The jacket lapel should contain a number of badges, of which one must be CND. An NUM badge is especially good, but don't try wearing it unless you're actually a member of that union. You can do so after you become an MP, when sucking up to the miners becomes obligatory. Then you can wear the union emblem even if the nearest you've been to the coal industry is the back of Arthur Scargill's Rover. Hand-made jumpers and corduroys are not absolutely essential among the Liberals, despite what people say, and David Steel has done very nicely in those striped shirts with white collars.

As far as background is concerned, don't fall for type-casting. A struggle from the gutter and a bit of trade unionism can work wonders in the Conservative Party, while privilege and wealth is not invariably a handicap for Labour aspirants. How do you think it is that the Labour Party has something of a tradition of public-school leaders while the last two Conservative Prime Ministers went to grammar schools?

The rule here is as follows ...

Reader: It's not the background that counts, it's how you use it.

Patrick Hannan: Remember, if there's one thing above all of which political parties hate to be accused it's prejudice. So when you go down to your Conservative selection conference, don't forget to hawk your working-class credentials like an encyclopedia salesman.

Reader: This great party of ours, ladies and gentlemen, draws its support from all sections of society – that is one of the qualities that makes it so great. My own origins are humble enough – but I am proud of them. My father was a miner, but he was determined to see that I had all the advantages in life that hard work could bring. The closure of his pit was, indeed, a blessing in disguise. He borrowed a little money and took over a tiny newsagent's shop. From five in the morning until late at night he and my mother worked to provide enough money for me to go to the local direct-grant grammar school. I repaid their dedication with my own so that I went on to university and later into the City. It is that tradition of self-help, of self-reliance, that once made this country great and will do so again. It is the determination not to be nannied by the Welfare State, the freedom that allows people to fend for themselves, that will once again bring admiration from the rest of the world. I am sure my parents would agree, if they were alive to hear me now.

Patrick Hannan: Pass the Kleenex, Fiona. Meanwhile, at the Labour selection meeting, you might think that the assembled brothers and sisters would be unsympathetic towards your privileged background. Not a bit of it.

Reader: It is only through an accident of birth, comrades ...

Patrick Hannan: Don't forget to say comrades ...

Reader: It's only through an accident of birth, comrades, that I have been given those opportunities which have been so cruelly denied to others by the pernicious class system which even now this government is trying to strengthen. If my father hadn't been a stockbroker, then I doubt if I could have shown the same courage and strength as many of our brothers and sisters who have overcome the obstacles put in their way by the establishment. But it's because I have experienced these things at first hand that I feel especially qualified to be of service to this constituency, and to this great movement of ours.

Patrick Hannan: By the way, for goodness' sake don't confuse this great movement of ours and this great party of ours ...

Reader: I know the iniquities of the public school system where the best education is bought, bought, yes bought, rather than provided according to need. I know, too, about the exploitation of workers unscrupulously carried out by private enterprise, the way in which our so-called captains of industry are lining their own pockets while oppressing those who create the wealth for them. Comrades, of course we must besiege the walls of capitalism from without, but we must also undermine them from within. With your support and confidence I am sure that to-gether ...

Patrick Hannan: And so on for as long as it takes. Just don't forget to mention Aneurin Bevan and Keir Hardie and the Spanish Civil War, if you can manage it. Anyway, if you've got a choice of background, the best rule is ...

Reader: Humble origins are best and should be milked for all they're worth.

Recording of Margaret Thatcher: We had a very, very, very large zinc bath and we had to heat the water to pour into it. And we did. But, you know, looking back, it really is fascinating. We used to have that, and there was a big room we kept for that. I say big room, it seemed large to me at the time, it wouldn't now. And we had a big coal fire.

●

I daresay a lot of MPs can lay claim to humble origins like that. I would not be surprised if Roy Hattersley's house had a tin bath by a coal fire when he was young. These days he is used to finer things and so is his mother.

Mrs Enid Hattersley became Lord Mayor of Sheffield, and when Ray Gosling was looking for a beloved Lord Mayor of a great British city for his Radio 4 series called *In the House of* . . . she agreed to invite him into her parlour. Clearly a woman of courage as well as character, she then allowed Gosling to spend the day watching her at her mayoral duties. The two of them had a high old time of it, driving about in the mayoral limousine, entertaining ambassadors, wining and dining.

The key man in the mayoral operation, it seems, is the secretary – in Mrs Hattersley's case Mr Straw, with whom she did not always see eye to eye.

Ray Gosling: Mr Straw is impeccably dressed in pin-stripe trousers and a most correct black jacket with four little cloth-covered buttons to the sleeve. A man nearing retirement and a municipal pension. A Jeeves. No, that's not right really. He's the permanent civil servant to changing Lord Mayors, and he brings the morning mail, which today includes the latest episode in a saga of correspondence to do with some missionary from Kitwe, that's in Zambia – the copper belt – who wants to call on the Mayor in her parlour on 11 September.

Straw: On the 11 September you will probably be in London with the Russians.

Hattersley: Oh dear . . .

Straw: He wants to come on 11 September and . . .

Hattersley: Well, how long's he staying?

Straw: I don't know. Remember he was also talking about the two ladies who supported him . . .

Hattersley: Yes, who were nice. Well, they were all nice. Jolly intelligent people.

Straw: He's not heard . . . yes . . . he's not heard from either of them. And he now writes to say that he understood that they were both very ill with cancer. So they probably don't want to see . . .

Hattersley: That's a double misfortune, isn't it?

Straw: Yes.

Hattersley: It's like Oscar Wilde ...

Straw: I've made some inquiries ...

Hattersley: '... it's sad to have lost one parent, but to have lost them both,' you know ...

Straw: I'll make some inquiries about them and see if they're still there.

Hattersley: Yeah ...

Straw: And if anyone knows them ...

Hattersley: Um ... excuse me, just one minute.

(She takes the diary.)

Hattersley: If they could get in, say, 12 September, we should be here.

Straw: That's right.

Hattersley: They could meet the Russians too. That would be very good. That's another inducement, isn't it? If you could let them know ...

Straw: I'll write ...

Hattersley: Right ... good. Do that, Mr Straw, please.

Ray: A test in composition for Mr Straw later in the day. The star correspondence dealt with, next was to cast an eye on the seating arrangements for lunch.

Straw: There's your table plan for today. I think you know everyone on it.

Hattersley: Mr Straw ... he's very good at the seating arrangements. I never ... he gave me that so that he's protecting himself. The Lord Mayor's seen it. But I wouldn't dream of interfering ... I wouldn't be good at protocol. I've never been able to determine who the right people are. Mr Straw is very good.

Straw: I'm very good ... at knowing who the right people are. *(Laugh)*

Ray: The table plan had in fact already been duplicated. There'd even been a copy for me. Enid looked up – maybe she knew what I was thinking.

Hattersley: Teaches you patience. That's the only virtue I claim. I'm a patient woman. Look how I suffer Mr Straw. Never a word … *(laugh)* … yeah … yeah …

Straw: The Ambassador will be presenting you with a box of your favourite material – mother-of-pearl.

Hattersley: My God.

Straw: So I gather.

Ray: This turned out to be a joke in bad taste because Enid's favourite material certainly is not mother-of-pearl. She'd just had to veto a mother-of-pearl set of caviar forks some lunatic suggested the City of Sheffield present to the Prince of Wales. Caviar forks from the most consistently socialist city in the British Isles! Somebody was pulling somebody's leg. Enid had thrown up in horror and she didn't like the design. It was horrible – to happen to her, an ex-chairman of the College of Art. But she doesn't want to hurt. So if she had to receive this personal gift of mother-of-pearl she'd have to receive mother-of-pearl. Too late to change now. And she wouldn't hurt an Ambassador.

●

Casting all such serious and worthy thoughts aside, let's turn to what they call a 'party quickie' on the Radio 4 comedy programme *Don't Stop Now … It's Fundation.* This one was written by John Langdon.

'Ere, I just found a couple of spare birds. Both blondes, twenty-two and single!

No, you go ahead without me.

Come on, what's wrong with that?

I'm into adultery these days.

So what's stopping you?

Nothing. I'm waiting for Mrs Right.

●

A rather more serious look at the consequences of adultery was taken in a *Forty Minutes* documentary on BBC2. It was an examination of what it is like to be 'the other woman', the mistress in a man's life. Three very different women spoke frankly about the situation. One of them clearly enjoyed the freedom of having a man around only now and then; another had had a baby by her lover and was coping with that; the third had been badly hurt when she was left by a man who went back to his wife. All of them in their own ways had had to come to terms with being second best.

Lady 1: Usually at the beginning of the week one has to say, 'Well, what nights are you free?' because, you know, he has to fit in the other woman – his wife. But otherwise we see each other as often as possible. I don't really want to see him every day, you know, because I have other things to do and other friends to see and other work to do. So, as he's rather an intense man, three or four days a week at the most is enough – that's why I like being a mistress.

Lady 3: It ended rather sadly and unfortunately and not at all as we both planned. We'd had a pact that we'd never finish on paper, and force of circumstance made it finish on paper. She found, in fact, a very innocent letter looking for a cheque book and it was quite normal for her to, when she needed it, because they were in a foreign country, to actually go and get it. And he would have to get it for her because the drawer was locked. On this particular occasion she went to get the cheque book and found the drawer open and unfortunately, in pulling out the cheque book, fell across the letter, which fortunately in fact didn't say very much – it just made it very clear that he knew somebody quite well in Brussels.

Interviewer: But do you think perhaps he wanted the wife to find the letter?

Lady 3: No, I'm sure not, quite sure. It was going far too well.

Interviewer: And what happened after that?

Lady 3: A very dramatic five lines arrived and I collected the letter and rushed back into bed to read it with great excitement, and I opened it and I was just shattered. After such an idyllic relationship, an undated, virtually unsigned five lines.

Interviewer: And what did the letter say?

Lady 3: So and so's found out – I can't remember exactly, but it was the equivalent of that. We've decided we've got to look closer into our relationship – I'm shellshocked – don't be worried for me. And, you know, his immediate reaction was thinking of himself.

Interviewer: But he never thought about you?

Lady 3: He knew that I would worry about how things would go when she did find out, but, no, there wasn't any effort to find out afterwards how I'd reacted.

Interviewer: Do you think it's worth the pain then?

Lady 3: Yes, that was. It was a year I'll never forget.

Lady 2: Well, suddenly you become a mother, and to a certain extent you come to understand the wife of the man that you're with because, you're not on a par with her, but you're part way in the same situation. I mean, my man was very good to me – I didn't really want for anything – he took care of us. Whatever we needed, she was provided for. But the whole relationship changed, and I wouldn't say for the better.

If a mistress has a child, it puts a completely different outlook on the situation. She's no longer a mistress – and suddenly the running away from the family to the mistress for that break, you're suddenly running to another family. He'd wanted to tell his wife – I didn't want him to. I didn't want anybody else to get hurt; there was no point in anybody else getting hurt. The relationship had gone on for a number of years on and off. The little daughter was here but why hurt other people by coming out with the relationship which in the finish he did tell her.

Interviewer: And do you ever see yourself getting into a similar relationship again?

Lady 2: No. Definitely not.

Interviewer: Why not?

Lady 2: I wouldn't want the hurt again. I don't want to be second best again. You know, next time, if there is a next time, I'm not going to have the crumbs, I'm going to have the cake.

●

Barnes' People on Radio 3 presents a series of short duologues written by Peter Barnes. He clearly has wonderful imagination because his conversations are always based on the bizarrest of themes. They have attracted some classy performers, including Sir John Gielgud, Joan Plowright, Peter Ustinov and Paul Schofield.

The two actresses cast to play Betty and Carol in Moondog Rogan and the Mighty Hamster were Eileen Atkins and Barbara Leigh Hunt. I bet they were glad it was only on radio!

(The sound of grunts and thuds as two women wrestlers, Carol 'Mighty Hamster' Fontaine and Betty 'Moondog' Rogan, practise wrestling holds in a ring.)

Betty: A Junkyard arm and hair whip. *(Carol is heard careering backwards.)* Rebound fast from the ropes. *(Carol is heard coming forward.)* A Bull Ventura shoulder block and stun. *(Carol grunts as if stunned.)* Repeat three Junkyard whips, rebounds and Ventura blocks. On the fourth, leg-dive me. *(Carol is heard sliding between Betty's legs.)* I fall to a flying head-scissors. *(She falls.)* You give me a Ripper Elliot headlock. *(She grunts and gasps as Carol applies a headlock on her.)*

Carol: Three Junkyard whips and Ventura blocks, a leg-dive, flying head-scissors and Ripper headlock. Make it four Junkyard whips and I'll leg-dive on the fifth. The more action-packed we make it the better. Be careful on the Junks. The last time I used that move Pretty-Girl Sommers took out a handful of my hair. Let's practise some hand-holds.

(There are grunts and the sounds of strain as they practise.)

Betty: If they paid Pretty-Girl Sommers what she was worth, she'd starve to death. I never liked working with her, never trusted her. Mind you, I've never trusted my milkman or my solicitor but the bird in my head tells me you've got to be able to trust your opponent otherwise you end up busted. When you headlock me remember I've got a bad ear.

Carol: I've got a dislocated shoulder and a chipped elbow. Have you got any more injuries I should know about besides the ear?

Betty: Three cracked ribs, elbow and knees broken, cartilage gone, back strained, eardrum split – just minor things. Outside the ring is where I really got hurt. But those injuries don't show. Trouble is, out there you never know when, where or who's going to hit you so you can't take precautions ... You move very evenly. I used to move like that once – as if I was going to fly.

Carol: I'm supposed to come into the ring tomorrow night in white satin. I don't mind putting on the little furry ears or even the whiskers – after all I am the 'Mighty Hamster'. *(She makes squeaking sound.)* Tsk – tsk – tsk. But a six-foot-long tail is going a bit far. How've they got you dressed as 'Moondog' Rogan?

Betty: The usual. Black satin, chains, black gloves and heavy black eye-shadow – and I howl. I howl for the moon, aawwwhh. They hear the 'moondog' howling and are supposed to run for their lives, aawwhh. I'm the heavy, in case you didn't notice, mad and bad under the moon's astral influence, aawwhh. I'm supposed to pick up a chair and throw it at the ref, preferably with him still in it. That's our promoter's idea – Herbie Greenslade'd make his crippled grandmother strip if there was money in it. When he suggested it I should've laughed in his face but why should I show him a good time for nothing? Give Herbie Greenslade a free hand and he'll stick it right in your back ... Let's get the feel of some hammerlocks ...

(They are heard grunting and gasping as they apply hammerlocks on each other in succession.)

•

Michael Bentine in a one-man show on Radio 2 plays all the characters. This sometimes becomes enormously complex and must take him ages to do. Here, however, is an example of one of his simpler, one-line gags.

(Scratching quill pen on parchment paper, with Florentine music on the lute in background.)

Writer (reading words as he writes): My dear Lucretia Borgia . . .
last night's party was delightful . . . the dinner was superb . . . I so
enjoyed the mushrooms . . . Aagh!

(Body falls on floor.)

●

You do not have to be a Borgia for sinister things to happen round about
you. Quite ordinary people in quite ordinary situations can suddenly find
that all is not as tranquil as it might seem. For a poetry programme on
Radio 3 on the subject of houses, Patric Dickinson found this strange little
piece by William Plomer called 'The Dorking Thigh'.

About to marry and invest
Their lives in safety and routine
Stanley and June required a nest
And came down on the 4.15.

The agent drove them to the Posh Estate
And showed them several habitations.
None did. The afternoon got late
With questions, doubts, and explanations.

Then day grew dim and Stan fatigued
And disappointment raised its head,
But June declared herself intrigued
To know where that last turning led.

It led to a Tudor snuggery styled
'Ye Kumfi Nooklet' on the gate.
'A gem of a home,' the salesman smiled,
'My pet place on the whole estate;

'It's not quite finished, but you'll see
Good taste itself.' They went inside.
'This little place is built to be
A husband's joy, a housewife's pride.'

They saw the white convenient sink,
The modernistic chimneypiece,
June gasped for joy, Stan gave a wink
To say, 'Well, here our quest can cease.'

99

The salesman purred (he'd managed well)
And June undid a cupboard door.
'For linen,' she beamed. And out there fell
A nameless Something on the floor.

'Something the workmen left, I expect,'
The agent said, as it fell at his feet,
Nor knew that his chance of a sale was wrecked.
'Good heavens, it must be a joint of meat!'

Ah yes, it was meat, it was meat all right,
A joint those three will never forget —
For they stood alone in the Surrey night
With the severed thigh of a plump brunette ...

        *   *   *

Early and late, early and late,
Traffic was jammed round the Posh Estate,
And the papers were full of the Dorking Thigh
And who, and when, and where, and why.

A trouser button was found in the mud
(Who made it? Who wore it? Who lost it? Who
   knows?)
But no one found a trace of blood
Or her body or face, or the spoiler of those.

He's acting a play in the common air
On which no curtain can ever come down.
Though 'Ye Kumfi Nooklet' was shifted elsewhere
June made Stan take a flat in town.

●

It is curious how some inventions are well documented and patented and others are not. Alexander Graham Bell invented the telephone, but who was the first person to think of the bicycle? According to an enchanting BBC2 programme on the history of the velocipede with the ingenious title of *Bicycle Clips*, the Russians claimed to have been the first to have invented it, but then it could have been Leonardo da Vinci. Actually, the evidence seemed to come down in favour of the French, and not all Frenchmen liked the invention.

First testy Frenchman: Paris is just now afflicted with a serious nuisance ... velocipedes, machines like the ghosts of departed spiders, on which horrible boys and detestable men career about the streets and boulevards.

Fashionable Frenchwoman: The velocoman, as he styles himself, is to be seen in all his glory, careering at full speed through the shady avenues of the Bois de Boulogne or skimming like some gigantic dragonfly over the level surface of the roads intersecting the Champs-Elysées.

Second testy Frenchman: Velocipedists are imbeciles on wheels.

Dorothy Richardson: On a bicycle you feel a different person; nothing can come near you, you forget who you are. Aren't you glad you are alive today when all these things are happening?

Rose Macaulay: We're all doing it now. It's glorious; the nearest approach to wings permitted to men and women here below. Intoxicating! And it's transforming clothes. Short jackets and cloth caps are coming in. Bustles are no more. And, my dear — bloomers are to be seen in the land.

Who's **YOUR** tailor?

Fair cyclist (wearing rational dress): Is this the wear to Wareham, please?

Native: Yes, miss, yew seem to me to ha got 'em on all right!

Northern doctor: In young girls the bones of the pelvis are not able to resist the tension required to ride a bicycle, and so many become more or less distorted in shape.

Punch *poet*:

> Yes, knickers are the proper dress
> Wherewith a cycle's seat to press;
> Convenient, and – should you be thrown –
> Making less re-ve-la-ti-on.

●

Although Elizabeth I died childless and her own childhood was harrowing to say the least, she seems to have had an especial concern for the welfare of young people. The boy choristers who sang for her in the Chapel Royal attracted her particular attention.

In a Radio 3 series called *The Gentlemen of the Chapel Royal*, Gordon Reynolds quoted a letter of hers which showed the minute interest she took in making sure that her choristers were well looked after. When their voices broke, they were either sent to another school or to Oxford or Cambridge, or found some other kind of job suitable to their talents and training.

This letter was addressed to the Dean and Chapter of Wells, who were reluctant to re-employ one of the Wells boys after he had spent some time in the Chapel Royal choir. His term there was finished and now the Queen was asking the Dean to take him back.

Reader: Trusty and well beloved, we greet you well. Whereas John Pitcher, sometime a chorister of your Church of Wells, was from thence brought hither to serve us in the room of a Child of our Chapel, in which place he hath remained nigh this six years, diligent in service, and to our good liking, till now his voice beginneth to change, he is not become so fit for our service, and herewith understanding that there is a singing-man's room void in the said church, we have thought it meet to recommend him unto you to be placed in the same, with our express command-ment that, according to the orders of your house, ye do admit and place him, the said John Pitcher, into the room of a singing-man in the said church, with all manner of houses, lodging, pays, duties and commodities whatsoever to the room of a singing-man there appertaining and belonging, to be had and perceived by him during his life, in as large and ample a manner as any other singing-man there now hath and enjoyeth for and in respect of his room.

Gordon Reynolds: The Queen certainly dotted the i's and crossed the t's. She regarded herself as being *in loco parentis*, and the choristers were known as the Children of the Chapel Royal.

•

A musical detective story was unravelled by the BBC World Service programme *Outlook*. In an Ulster attic an unpublished manuscript of a Mass by Josef Haydn was found. John Tidmarsh pieced together the story with the help of the noted Haydn expert Professor H. C. Robbins Landon and John McClintock, the man in whose attic the lost manuscript was found.

John McClintock: It was found just in the cupboard over there. I'd known there was a thing connected with music – a folder which had been collected by my great aunt, and she'd got all these listed. There are quite a number of facsimiles and she'd listed them as facsimiles. But she hadn't put any comment against the Haydn at all. So I didn't think very much of it. Well, I never really thought that there would be anything of particular value. I mean, one imagines, at least I imagined in my ignorance, that a composer composes music and hands it over to whoever wants to play it; it's played, and everybody knows about it. It didn't strike me that it might be a manuscript that had never been played and had got lost, as this one apparently has.

John Tidmarsh: Well, ultimately the London auctioneers Christie's sought to authenticate the Haydn manuscript, and they called in Professor H. C. Robbins Landon, of University College, Cardiff. He's been telling Martin Wylliams exactly what happened.

H. C. Robbins Landon: Well, I'm lying in my little bed minding my own business reading the newspapers just before Christmas, and the phone rings, and on the other end is my old friend Alby Rosenthal. Now Alby is an antiquarian-music dealer; in other words, he goes to the auctions, usually with orders from the great libraries, and they say, we want this piece by a person, and he obtains it for them. And he said, 'Robby, I've just come from a cocktail party at Christie's. They've received a shipment of stuff from Northern Ireland and they were all excited about a Beethoven, so they showed me the Beethoven, and on the left of the Beethoven I saw a big Haydn manuscript. As they were chattering in my ear about the Beethoven, I looked at the Haydn and it's the lost *Sunt Bona Mixta Malis*.' So I said in my usual forthright American way, 'Christ.' And he said, 'You may well say that.' So he said, 'Look, I'll arrange for you to go up and have a proper look at it and tell them what it's all about, because they don't really know what it is — it just arrived.' So I arranged all this with Christie's. My wife and I had a nice meal at the top of Fortnum and Mason and toasted Papa Haydn with a glass of champagne, then we got into a taxi and went to Christie's. We were led into the bowels of Christie's and there was a very pretty young woman called Kate Hedworth, who said, 'There it is, Professor Landon.' So I looked at all of this, looked at the hallmarks and everything, and there was no doubt about it. There was the manuscript that we knew had existed. We knew all about it, in fact, except where it was.

Martin Wylliams: When you say there was no doubt about it at all — I mean, how do you authenticate something like that?

H. C. Robbins Landon: Well, the whole thing was in Haydn's handwriting. It's signed by Haydn on the first page, *Giuseppe Haydn, 1768*, and it starts '*In Nomine Domini*', 'In the Name of the Lord', in the way all Haydn's manuscripts do, and it even, in this case, has the sign of the cross on the front as well, Haydn being a pious man.

•

There was nothing particularly pious about those two great opera stars Dame Nellie Melba and Enrico Caruso. They were not above playing practical jokes upon one another even when in the middle of a serious piece of work.

Martin Mayer, historian of the Metropolitan Opera in New York, told this story about them in a Radio 4 programme.

Melba chewed gum, and before she went on stage she would stick it to a piece of glass in the backstage area. And once Caruso substituted a wad of chewing-tobacco for her gum. I mean, he would do things like that. Even in Monte Carlo, when he was still a kid, he brought a toy mouse to the last act of *Bohème* and squeaked it in her ear while she was dying – making it terribly hard for her to die without giggling.

•

Regular listeners to Radio 4's *Just a Minute* programme will know that, according to the format invented by Ian Messiter, contestants must speak on a given subject without hesitation, repetition or deviation, and they must keep that up for the space of one minute.

The rules are open to all sorts of interpretations by the chairman, Nicholas Parsons, and by the others taking part. Sometimes the audience is called upon to arbitrate in a particularly difficult decision, but usually a good time is had by all.

In one vintage edition the subject was Limericks. The result, as you can imagine, was an absolute riot, with buzzers being pressed right, left and centre in the competition to get another, even naughtier limerick onto the programme. Those taking part were Kenneth Williams, Derek Nimmo, Peter Jones and, to start, Brian Johnston.

Johnston: I'm not very fond of limericks, possibly because I can't make them up. I find it very difficult to get the two middle lines, and the last line is always a bit too *(buzzer)* ...

Parsons: Um, Peter Jones has challenged.

Jones: Repetition of 'line'.

Parsons: Yes, I know.

Nimmo: No, it was 'line' and 'lines' ...

Parsons: 'Line' and 'lines' ...

Johnston: I said 'line' and 'lines'.

Parsons: That's right, you're, you're ... you did two different words there and we have to listen very carefully. So you have another point for a wrong challenge, fifty-one seconds on Limericks, Brian, starting now.

Johnston: Very often the end is very rude and something you couldn't *(buzzer)* mention here.

Parsons: Er, Kenneth Williams.

Williams: Two 'verys'.

Parsons: Yes, you said that. You said you find it very difficult and this was ... right. So, er, Kenneth has the subject of Limericks and there are forty-seven seconds starting now.

Williams: There was a young lady of Ryde who ate a green apple and died. The fruit fermented inside the lamented and made cider inside her inside. *(Laughter/applause.) (Buzzer.)*

Parsons: Brian Johnston.

Johnston: Inside her.

Parsons: I do think you did repeat the word 'inside'. Thirty-seven seconds, Brian, with you starting now.

Johnston: Some lirry ... oh! *(Laughter.) (Buzzer.)*

Parsons: Derek.

Nimmo: Hesitation.

Parsons: I know. Isn't it rotten? It's so difficult playing ...

Johnston: It's my teeth. *(Laughter.)*

Parsons: Thirty-five seconds on Limericks, Derek, starting now.

Nimmo: There was an old poof of Khartoum, who took a lesbian up to his room. They lay on the bed and suddenly said, 'Who does what, with what and to whom?' *(Laughter/applause.) (Buzzer.)* I'm sorry. Shall I go on, Mr Chairman, can I continue?

Parsons: Lord – excuse me. Just a moment. Lord Reith, turn in your grave. *(Laughter.)* Brian Johnston challenged you and we'd like to know what it was, Brian.

Johnston: Well, there were two 'whats'. *(Laughter.)*

Parsons: And I should think there were! *(Laughter.)* In that situation there were more than a few but, er ...

Nimmo: Oh, right.

Parsons: Derek, I think you've broken ... new ice in the realms of the history of broadcasting and if you want to write to us about them, please address your letters personally to Derek Nimmo, 'cos you will get a personalized reply *(laughter)*, um, with another limerick perhaps ... Derek, you get the subject back and there are twenty-one seconds on Limericks starting now.

Nimmo: There was a young lady from Colesville who sat herself down on a moleshill, the inquisitive mole stuck his nose and ... *(Laughter.) (Buzzer.)* ... May I retire, I think *(laughter)* before I'm made forcibly redundant.

Williams: I think he ill– ... I think he illustrated Brian's point about being difficult to finish your limerick, didn't he? *(Laughter.)*

Parsons: Yes ... yes, I think some of them shouldn't have been started actually. *(Laughter.)* Peter Jones, I'm pleased to say, got in on this round, 'cos we might get one from him. So, Peter, yes, a correct challenge. I don't know what for, but it sounded correct *(laughter)* ... came to a shuddering halt, we're delighted to say. Twelve seconds on Limericks starting now.

Jones: There was a young man of Torbay, when sailing to China one day was lashed to the tiller by a sex-crazed gorilla and the Far East is a very long way. *(Laughter ... whistle. Applause.)*

●

For Seult Cunyngham-Brown, who was held captive by the Japanese for three and a half years during the last war, the Far East meant a prison camp.

Cunyngham-Brown was one of the old Far East hands to talk to Charles Allen for the Radio 4 series *Last Tales from the South China Seas*. He had been in the Malayan civil service, but with Japanese incursions into Southeast Asia he had been called up to active duty as a member of the Royal Naval Volunteer Reserve.

Eventually he fled from Singapore by sea in a small boat, dodging bombs and getting as far as the islands north of Sumatra before being captured and imprisoned by the Japanese. They sentenced him to death but he narrowly missed that by being shipped off to build a railroad – which, as we have heard from many other sources, was a kind of living death. Cunyngham-Brown, however, was a resourceful man and not above digging about in rubbish bins for food to keep body and soul together. He was one of the lucky ones who survived, and when the war was ended by the dropping of the atomic bombs on Nagasaki and Hiroshima, he and his fellow prisoners were still working in their prison camp.

As soon as we heard that the war was over, aircraft began to come over in increasing numbers and fly over the camp. Three miles away there was a field that had been an airstrip at one time, and I got the job from the camp commandant to repair the airstrip with a hundred men.

Every day these three large aircraft came lower and lower. One, leading the flight, was a very polished-looking machine indeed, and to my horror one day it looked as though it really was going to land far earlier than it should; we hadn't cleared the bushes from the end of the runway. I told everybody to scatter quick – I thought it was coming in – scrammed to the sides, they all ran to the sides as hard as they could. The thing touched down in a shower of dust, sprang into the air again and touched down again with another wallop, and finally scuttered off as it slowed up into this scrub and bushes at the end of the airstrip. It turned itself round and came back along the airstrip. I was furious of course, and ran after them to say, For God's sake, don't let the other aircraft come in, you'll, you'll have a crash, wait another three days. But as I ran my loincloth fell off – with my feet bound in sackcloth, no other stitch of clothing on me, in a furious temper, and a long beard *(laugh)*. I was prepared to yell at the pilot, but I stopped, transfixed, because the door opened, the ladder came down. At the top stood somebody looking like a Wren, but actually I found later it was the St John Ambulance Brigade uniform, and a very handsome young lady began to descend the ladder. I stood at the bottom and could only say, I do beg your pardon. She said, My dear, it's perfectly all right, what you need is a cigarette, and opening a gold cigarette case she offered me one – which I took with avidity, I may add. We thereupon walked across towards where the lorries were. She said, Take me to your camp at once, please. I said, Yes – er, by the way, who are you, what is your name? She said, I am Lady Mountbatten.

●

Earlier fragments from our colonial past in Asia were gathered together for

108

a BBC World Service programme called *The Tiger Trap*, presented by Christopher Nicholson. It was a celebration of the great cat of Asia – the tiger.

Now protected by conservation laws, the tiger was at one time mercilessly pursued by white hunters. On the backs of elephants, on tree platforms, they waited with loaded rifles. The more intrepid of them pursued the poor beasts on foot, but that was asking for trouble. F. R. Hicks, one of the most renowned of nineteenth-century hunters, nearly met his end in this way.

I was poking about among a lot of stunted palm bushes when suddenly there was a terrific roar and I was conscious that the wounded tigress was in midair coming straight for my head. I had only time to throw up my rifle and pull both barrels simultaneously, when I was knocked flat on the ground with the tiger on top of me. My shot had however for a moment knocked her senseless, and as soon as I realized this I jumped to my feet and tried to reload my empty rifle. But alas! my pockets had been ripped open by the claws of the tigress and were lying at my feet; and before I discovered this fact, the tiger recovered her senses. I

had no time to pick up even one of the precious cartridges, for she at once reared herself up against me with a fierce gurgling snarl, while I just for a moment held her off by the throat and frantically searched with one hand the corners of my pocket in the despairing hope of finding just one cartridge; but the next moment I was down with the terrible brute on top of me.

What happened after that I am not quite certain ... When I came to, my first sensation was of being suffocated by some heavy weight, which I found to be the body of the tigress. My left hand was a pulp of raw flesh and broken or crushed bones; a portion of my left hip had been torn out; my boots were full of blood. In fact, I was covered with blood from head to toe, mostly my own and partly that of the tiger. In this state I started to totter as best I could towards camp, which lay over three miles away. I believe some of my men joined me, two of whom then supported me. It seems that when the tigress attacked most of them had bolted to camp, where they informed my wife I had been killed. That brave woman snatched up a loaded gun and started to my rescue. Apparently my conscience pricked me, for I am told that when I saw my wife coming towards me I made my supporters stand off, while I lit a cigar and, putting my left hand behind my back, met her jauntily whistling a tune as if nothing had happened – though my boots, by squelching with blood, gave the show away rather.

●

Bravery of another kind, in the face of death, was shown by a young Indian girl called Gitanjali. Her story was told by James Cameron in a Radio 4 programme.

Gitanjali spent most of her young life suffering from cancer. Although she knew that she was dying, she wanted to conceal the fact from her family and friends for fear of their sympathy. Secretly she wrote about her feelings in verse and hid her poems about the house, inside books or cupboards or amongst clothes. Her mother found them after her death. Not all the poems were sad, but in this one, called 'The Moment of Truth', she faces what it will be like to die and what it will mean to those closest to her in life.

Gitanjali is dead
Gitanjali is dead
People are whispering around

110

A horror of shock
But the moment of truth
That's all
It's all about.

Foolish are those
Who shed tears
Mingled with sorrow and pain
Little do they realise
The joy that is mine
Free of torture
Free of pain
And free of guilt
That shook my faith.

I am now at the threshold
Of my life to start afresh
A new lease of life ...

The time stands still
The eternity has passed
Gitanjali the child has passed
The mother looks down
Upon the much loved
Blood drained face
Tears trickling down her face
Go my love, go my child
She sighs

I'll be sad
I'll be lonely
I'll be miserable without you
But I'm glad and thankful
To Him the merciful that ...
At least you my child are at rest.

●

Another sad duty fell to James Cameron when he was asked to speak on Radio 4 about his old friend and colleague René Cutforth, at the time of his death.

Cameron and Cutforth were both consummate reporters. They belong, as the programme said, to the heroic age of foreign reporting. They covered many stories together, among them the flight of the Dalai Lama from Tibet. It was from that period that James Cameron recalled a memorable sidelight on the personality of René Cutforth.

He had a kind of persecution feeling at that particular time. He had an idea that he was being watched very carefully by the secret police, which to some degree was true, though nothing like the way he thought it. And everywhere he went he'd look around to see whether he was being followed and so and so on. And it became very, very troublesome. Well, eventually, we got rid of the story and we went back to Calcutta, where we got the first bed we'd had for a long time. We got adjoining rooms in the Grand Hotel there and we went to bed. Early in the morning I was wakened up by René, who had come into my room in a state of serious emotion. He said, 'Sorry, James, I knew it would happen, but they've caught up with me at last.' I said, 'What the devil do you mean?' 'Well,' he said, 'there's a secret policeman in my room. He's disguised as a bearer, disguised as a waiter in a white coat. He keeps shaking me on the shoulder and saying "I took a look." So I asked him what he took a look at. And he won't tell me.' So I said, 'This is nonsense. I'll go.' And we both returned to his room. And, sure enough, there was a perfectly authentic hotel bearer hanging around with a cup of tea in his hand. I said, 'What on earth are you doing threatening my friend here?' 'Not threatening. Sahib asked to be called in morning. So I called. I said, "Eight o'clock, eight o'clock."' And his conscience, you see, interpreted, 'eight o'clock' as 'I took a look'. So that was the kind of neurosis he was capable of.

●

Baron Münchausen was the creation of a German professor, Rudolf Eric Raspe, who left his native land in some haste following a charge of embezzlement and settled in England in 1775. He based the character of Münchausen on a German soldier of fortune who was born in 1720, served with the Russian cavalry against the Turks and then, in 1760, retired to his family estates to regale all who would listen with fantastic tales of his adventures.

Donald Bancroft adapted the stories for Radio 3. In this one, Münchausen describes a shooting expedition in Ceylon, when he was accompanied by one of the governor's brothers.

Near the banks of a large piece of water, which had engaged my attention, I thought I heard a rustling noise behind; on turning about I was almost petrified (as who would not?) at the sight of a lion, which was evidently approaching with the intention of satisfying his appetite with my poor carcass, and that without asking my consent. What was to be done in this horrible dilemma? I had not even a moment for reflection; my piece was only charged with swan-shot, and I had no other about me; however, though I could have no idea of killing such an animal with that weak kind of ammunition, yet I had some hopes of frightening him by the report, and perhaps of wounding him also. I immediately let fly, without waiting till he was within reach; and the report did but enrage him, for he now quickened his pace and seemed to approach me full speed: I attempted to escape, but that only added to my distress; for the moment I turned about, I found a large crocodile, with his mouth extended almost ready to receive me: on my right hand was the piece of water before mentioned, and on my left a deep precipice, said to have a receptacle at the bottom for venomous creatures; in short, I gave myself up as lost, for the lion was now upon his hind-legs, just in the act of seizing me; I fell involuntarily to the ground with fear, and as it afterwards appeared, he sprang over me. I lay some time in a situation which no language can describe, expecting to feel his teeth or talons in some part of me every moment: after waiting in this prostrate situation a few seconds, I heard a violent but unusual noise, different from any sound that had ever before assailed my ears; nor is it at all to be wondered at, when I inform you from whence it proceeded: after listening for some time, I ventured to raise my head and look around, when, to my unspeakable joy, I perceived the lion had, by the eagerness with which he sprang at me, jumped forward as I fell, into the crocodile's mouth! which, as before observed, was wide open; the head of the one stuck in the throat of the other! and they were struggling to extract themselves! I fortunately recollected my hunting knife which was by my side; with this instrument I severed the lion's head at one blow, and the body fell at my feet! I then with the butt-end of my fowling-piece rammed the head farther into the throat of the crocodile and destroyed him by suffocation, for he could neither gorge nor eject it.

Soon after I had thus gained a complete victory over my two powerful adversaries, my companion arrived in search of me.

After mutual congratulations, we measured the crocodile, which was just forty feet in length.

●

A sadder and yet perhaps more truthful story from the East was told in another programme in *Last Tales from the South China Seas*, a series conceived and created by Michael Mason.

The series began by describing the idyllic last days of the empire in Southeast Asia in the words of people who were there. Then came the moment when British rule was abruptly swept away by the invasion of the Japanese, who overran the Malay peninsula and swept into Singapore.

It had been a peaceful corner of the empire but when the Japanese warlords made their move nothing would ever be the same again. Ships arrived to take off the women and children but not all of them got away. Dorothy Lucy was one who stayed behind.

Evening after evening Sir Strenton Thomas broadcasted that we were perfectly safe where we were, that we were to stay at our posts, that we were not to leave, and Peter and I agreed that we should be much happier if we were married and fought out the siege as a married couple rather than being on our own. Anyway we wanted to get married. My friend and I couldn't find any currants in Singapore, so I went to the Bishop of Singapore, Bishop Wilson, who was a great friend of mine and later so dreadfully tormented and tortured by the Japanese, and he and I sat in his air-raid shelter while he transferred a bag of currants into my lap for me to take off to make my wedding cake. And by the morning of 7 February 1942, exactly a week before Singapore fell, we were ready for the wedding. We put notices in the papers that were still being printed – the papers were being printed, everything was going on as normal. We asked all our friends and relations to come to Singapore Cathedral at 2.30 on the afternoon of 7 February. We had the organ, we had hymns, we were married by the archdeacon Graham White; bombs were falling all around us, but it was a perfectly beautiful wedding. We had a wedding reception with orchids all round us, and many friends came straight from the front, some with arms bound up, some with mud on their trousers and boots, many of whom of course we never saw again, and many of our women friends were lost at sea when their ships were bombed and sunk by the Japanese. But we had a very happy and glorious wedding and we went for our honeymoon to the hotel just outside Singapore. We spent the honeymoon in an air-raid shelter, because Singapore at that time was being bombed day and night. We had one more night together in my flat in Singapore and then Peter went back to the front line and I went back to Alexandra Hospital. Neither of us had any idea that it would be nearly four years before we saw each other again.

●

When doing national service, you did not necessarily reach the front line. You were much more likely to end up square-bashing or whitewashing stones or repeatedly cleaning your kit.

It's over twenty years since the last national serviceman left the army. Before that, from the end of the last war all young men who were fit enough were conscripted for a period of two years' service with the armed forces.

In a programme on BBC1 entitled *Called Up*, ex-national servicemen looked back at those years. This extract features Auberon Waugh, Monsignor Bruce Kent and the man who subsequently put his knowledge of army bull to such colourful use, the actor Windsor Davies.

Windsor Davies: There's the – an army boot, right, the good old army boot. Now then, as you can see, it's got mottled leather all over it. This is the same boot – I think it was issued in 1939 or even maybe before that. Now, if you notice there, you've got eyeholes. This is one part of the equipment I'm talking about. You've got eyeholes for the, um, laces, laceholes. You had to scrape the shellac off that, and not leave a speck, and then brasso the shi– you can see the brass there – and then brasso that. And all sorts of little activities like this. When you needed to get to sleep, you know.

Bruce Kent: There was a lot of mindlessness, when you think of the layout of the kit on the beds, where your laces had to be circled and polished and your tins and everything. It was a kind of religious approach to things, ritual. It was very mindless.

Windsor Davies: And you'd have guys cleaning floors with toothbrushes, and you'd think – I mean, that is the height of idiocy.

Auberon Waugh: We did have to weed a – a patch of lawn between the huts with our knives and forks, our eating irons. I remember that being quite humorous.

Even the most disastrous call-up stories seemed to have a funny side. Take this example from Ian Whitaker, who spent his national service in the RAF.

I arrived at this station and here was I, being paid, and they, they wanted to give a me job to do and they, they said, 'Oh, you're going to work in airfield control.' I said, 'Well, I don't know anything about airfield control.' 'Oh,' he said, 'there's nothing to it. You – nothing to it at all,' he said. 'You just go and sit in that caravan,' he said, 'and just spend several hours there, and then, when your time's up, you go back to your billet, and, and that's it.' I said, 'Well, what happens if . . . if something goes wrong?' He said, 'Oh, nothing can go wrong, but,' he said, 'if anything goes wrong, all you do is get that old pistol out there and fire it. It's a Very pistol,' he said, 'and fire a flare.' He said, 'If everything's all right, you can fire – fire this one,' he said, 'which fires a green flare. But,' he said, 'everything's always all right, so you'd better not waste, ah, the flare firing that. But,' he said, 'if anything goes wrong, you'd fire this one, which is a red flare.'

Ah, this particular day, when I was sitting in this caravan on the edge of the benighted airfield, I looked out of the window, and there was a Tiger Moth about to take off, you see, and at the same time there was one of these Harvards, which were a much faster aircraft, landing. I thought, my goodness if ... if this goes on there, there'll be two crashed aircraft in the middle of the runway. So I have to do something. So of course I thought of the instructions I'd received, which were to fire this flare. So I rushed to the side. I thought, I mustn't fire the green one, I must fire the red one, and, ah, I got this very cumbersome pistol, which was like some sort of blunderbuss almost – it was already loaded – and I stuck it out of the window and pulled the trigger, and of course, ah ah, the flare went shooting across. But what I didn't realize is that I had aimed at the aircraft that was taking off, you see, and thi– this, ah, flare went *whoosh* along the ground, or parallel with the ground, hit the aircraft which was just about to take off. Well, the thing was made of balsa wood and ... and ... and ... ah, very inflammable glue, I suppose, and canvas. And it, it just went shooting up in flames again. I ... I seemed to have a sort of arsonist's record in the Air Force. Anyway, ah, it went shooting up. The pilot jumped out – it ... it was a, it was a plane which had an open cockpit, he was able to get out. I suppose he was a bit shaken.

●

The troubles in Northern Ireland were the setting for a tragically moving play on Radio 3. *Never In My Lifetime*, written by Shirley Gee, told the story of a Belfast girl who fell in love with a British soldier and of the dilemma that faced them as a result.

Tessie had grown up with violence. She lived in a world where neighbours were blinded by rubber bullets, old school friends were as likely to be dealing out reprisals to those unfaithful to the cause as to be on the receiving end of them. Tom, the soldier, had the simple hope that his number would not come up if he hung on to his lucky rabbit's foot.

Tessie had already been warned about the dangers of the relationship, branded by her own people as that most hated of things, a 'soldier-lover'. Then her friend Maire urged her to join in with something that could prove her loyalty to the cause.

117

(Tessie's room. Night.)

Maire: It's just a wee job. Are you not Irish after all? Are you loyal? Prove it, then.

Tessie: What do they want us to do?

Maire: Smile. Act nice, dance a bit, string them along, you know.

Tessie: And then?

Maire: And then they'll come along and have a word.

Tessie: What are they after?

Maire: Inside information.

Tessie: They'll never get a thing from them.

Maire: Leave that to the lads.

Tessie: What'll they do to them?

Maire: Hurt them a bit maybe. That's all.

Tessie: Are you sure?

Maire: Sure I'm sure.

Tessie: I don't like to think of him hurt.

Maire: Look, you can help or you cannot, it's up to you. Only Kerry's a bit of a frightening fellow, I shouldn't care to argue with him myself.

Tessie: Oh, God, what'll I do?

Maire: Do what you're asked to. Tessie, it's just a knees-up, we've to get them there and entertain them until the lads arrive. Nothing more. What happens after isn't our affair.

Tessie: Just the sergeant and the other two, leave Tom out of it, why not?

Maire: Him most of all. Remember Mrs Cromerty. And Brendan. And God knows how many more of us.

Tessie: I can't. I can't.

Maire: Soldier-lover.

Tessie: Oh, Maire, please. Not Tom.

118

Maire: Tessie. It gets you off the hook. Kerry's a stickler for discipline. He's a loner – they don't approve of him, he can be a bit ferocious, it could be quite a bloody hook. Everything will work out fine – I'll be in for sure and you'll be right again. A clean slate. All forgotten.

Tessie: Maire? Not Tom.

Maire: All of them. Your squaddie too.

Tessie: Sweet Jesus, what'll I do?

Maire: You can't be in a war with your arms folded. You'll have to choose.

(The park. Dusk.)

Tom: I'd rather be alone with you than at this knees-up.

Tessie: Only for a while, then we could slip away.

Tom: OK then.

Tessie: And the others?

Tom: They'll leap at it. Booze and birds. No chance of them not coming.

Tessie: Nine o'clock then. Don't lose that address.

Tom: I won't. I won't.

Tessie: You're sure we can –

Tom: I've told you how we fiddle it twice. We'll make it. Barring any sudden aggro.

Tessie: That's great then. I must go.

Tom: You're really cunning, aren't you, Tess. You've set a trap for me, haven't you?

Tessie: What?

Tom: Lured me with your flashing eyes and your little boy's knees, that's what you've done. And I've fell right smack in. I've had it, haven't I.

Tessie: Tom, I –

Tom: I've bloody had it. I'm in love with you. Never thought I'd hear myself say that, not in cold blood sort of thing. Next thing I'll be asking you to marry me.

Tessie: Oh, Tom, it's no good for us, no good at all.

Tom: It's bloody marvellous, I'm not used to it, that's all. Hey, Tess, you're not supposed to cry, I'm telling you I love you. I thought you might be pleased. *(Tessie sobs.)* You're not pregnant, are you? Because if you are ...

Tessie: No.

Tom: I wouldn't mind, you know. I meant it.

Tessie: Oh, you're so stupid. No, I'm not pregnant.

Tom: Come here. Let's have a hold of you.

Tessie: You're very strong, aren't you.

Tom: Fit enough. Why?

Tessie (in a whisper): It's easy to die here.

Tom: Go on, get on home, put your fancy gear on for tonight. Roll on nine o'clock, then, eh?

Tessie: I left him. Barbed wire squeezing round my heart, the wind in my throat. I chose. Oh, God forgive me. I chose for Brendan, broken by fist and hood and hard white light. For Mrs Cromerty, the life almost blown out of her beneath her cloth. For Maggie Ryan, slit on the mouth and then between the legs. For me. For me. I chose in the park, our park, there in the snow, under the pale communion wafer of the sun. I lost my soul. I left him. Tom, with his bony knuckles and his rabbit's foot and his way of saying Tess. I looked back once and he was stood there watching me. Blowing on his cupped hands, changing feet, stamping. The soldiers stamp. When they slam their way up our streets, sparks fly from their boots struck off the pavements. Their eyes are iron, their teeth are broken glass ... I couldn't wave to him. I stood at the dark edge of the park and I looked back. My boots had made a trail of hell marks bitten into the snow, hard black holes. Like bullet holes. A trail that led straight back to him.

●

Religion continues to play a central role in the BBC's broadcasts. This is a legacy of Reithian principle and, though other faiths get a look in these days, Christianity still predominates.

A seasonal offering on Radio 4 is *In Praise of God*. In Advent, the programme looked forward to the nativity, and in so doing it took a fresh look at one of the main figures in the drama who so often gets pushed to the sidelines. The poem 'Joseph Speaks' was written by Neville Braybrooke.

I am tired of being thought of as an old man
Leaning upon a staff
My beard is not grey
Many miles did I pace the stable floor on the night of the
      birth —
And many more did I walk beside the ass bearing the Mother
      and Child
On our flight into Egypt

Yet when poets and painters came to tell my story they altered
      the facts
The painters gave my shoulders a stoop
And the poets shortened my stride to a shuffle

They were mistaken
They confused age with authority

My passions were those of any young Jew of my tribe
My senses as keen
From my bench I watched the shadow of my espoused grow
      fuller
Had I been deceived — and by whom?
Other women when found out have been stoned to death by
      the people
But at night in dreams I heard voices promising to make
      perfect the impossible

Sometimes the villagers spoke of two-headed goats
And of calves deformed at birth
I said nothing
I thought of the mysterious conception in my *own* house
Was I mistaken when I heard the beating of wings?
(There were nests in the trees nearby)

121

Words formed in my mind – and became a consolation 'Fear
    not, Joseph'
Where did they spring from?
For beware – Pride in the heart can nourish the imagination
So I said to my soul 'Be patient, be still'

The wings and the voices persisted
My confidence grew in the Word

The House of David would have a new Lord

●

James Fenton was not so full of good will in his poem about the Almighty
which was broadcast on Radio 3 in the series *The Living Poet*.

God, A Poem

A nasty surprise in a sandwich,
A drawing-pin caught in your sock,
The limpest of shakes from a hand which
You'd thought would be firm as a rock,

A serious mistake in a nightie,
A grave disappointment all round
Is all that you'll get from th'Almighty,
Is all that you'll get underground,

Oh he said: 'If you lay off the crumpet
I'll see you alright in the end.
Just hang on until the last trumpet.
Have faith in me, chum – I'm your friend.'

But if you remind him, he'll tell you:
'I'm sorry, I must have been pissed –
Though your name rings a sort of a bell. You
Should have guessed that I do not exist.

'I didn't exist at Creation,
I didn't exist at the Flood,
And I won't be around for Salvation
To sort out the sheep from the cud –

'Or whatever the phrase is. The fact is
In soteriological terms
I'm a crude existential malpractice
And you are a diet of worms.

'You're a nasty surprise in a sandwich.
You're a drawing-pin caught in my sock.
You're the limpest of shakes from a hand which
I'd have thought would be firm as a rock,

'You're a serious mistake in a nightie,
You're a grave disappointment all round –
That's all that you are,' says th'Almighty,
'And that's all that you'll be underground.'

●

One of the things Kate Tiffin highlighted in a programme she compiled
called *The Cat's Whiskers* was the fastidiousness of cats. Felines have
been with us for thirty-five million years so they have had time to learn a
thing or two, and in a story called *Jennie* by Paul Gallico the central
character, a stray London tabby, is quite happy to pass on some of her
knowledge. The object of her teaching is Peter, a boy who turns into a cat.
Jennie saves his life and then instructs him in how to comport himself
during the eight he has left.

123

When in doubt — any kind of doubt — wash! If you have committed any kind of error and anyone scolds you — wash. If you slip and fall off something and somebody laughs at you — wash. If you are getting the worst of an argument and want to break off hostilities until you have composed yourself, start washing. Remember, every cat respects another cat at her toilet. That's our first rule of social deportment, and you must also observe it.

Wisdom is something we always seem to associate with cats, but for the poet P. J. Kavanagh writing about his tabby cat, Copper, another quality was paramount.

She was brought to us, a stray kitten, by the local policeman. She grew into a good-looking cat with a particularly beautiful face, but what was most remarkable about her, and knowledge of it settled on us over the years, was her gentleness. Voles, young rats and the occasional weasel would not agree; but about the house she padded in stately fashion, with a low murmur of greeting if anyone addressed her, and when she was hungry she never asked for food but sat patiently by her plate until somebody noticed. Unbidden, she used to accompany us on long walks across the fields, a camouflaged shadow along the bottoms of the hedges. I never saw her claws unsheathed in anger even when painfully manhandled by children; she just went limp and waited for it to pass.

I took not much notice of her until one day I realised, so soothing was her presence that I drank peace from her. I seriously tried to learn from that aware self-containment. However apparently asleep, you only had to whisper her name and one ear would twitch, the one nearest the noise (no wasted effort) and she would stretch and purr and settle herself again.

●

A delightful essay about cats was read on Radio 3 during the interval of one of their concerts. *Cats in Council* was written by Mary Elizabeth Coleridge in 1907, the year of her death.

Two cats were once enjoying *The Merchant of Venice* together.

One was a stage cat. The actors and actresses were very fond of her, and she often sat in the prompter's box, on first nights especially.

'I acted once myself!' she said in a confidential whisper aside to her friend. 'It was in *Romeo and Juliet.* I have every sympathy with young love, and all my warmest feelings are stirred when the *jeune premier* knows how to climb like a cat, as Romeo does. But they talked about a lark and a nightingale until my mouth watered. It always does, you know, when I hear people say "What larks!" I thought there really must be a bird or two in that very stiff green tree that grows outside all the windows in Verona: so I ran across the stage as fast as ever I could. You have no conception of what it is to be on the stage. I never knew before what nervousness was. All those opera-glasses fixed upon one, all those restless, flashing human eyes! But I was a *succès fou.* With one scrabble of my paws, without even blotting a line, I changed a tragedy into a comedy. Every one laughed – even Romeo and Juliet, poor dear young things!'

'Ah!' said the parlour cat, who came from South Kensington,

and had attended Shakespeare Readings. She thought it rather a vulgar story really.

Still they were both cats of superior education, and a good play was an intellectual treat to both. It was *caviare* to them in the sense in which a good play was *caviare* to the Prince of Denmark, not to the general.

'Very odd,' said the patroness of the stage, 'how much there is in the work of Shakespeare that is of the deepest interest to cats. I sometimes think he must have been a cat himself. Every inch of fur on my tail stands on end when I hear the sentinel say, as he walks up and down at Elsinore, "Not a mouse stirring!" I know the little wretches. Depend upon it, there were six at least in the cellarage under his very nose, if he had only sniffed. Hamlet knew that well enough. "A rat – a rat in the arras!" That was what he was thinking of the whole time. That was why he went mad. It is a very strange thing that the critics should never have thought of it. He had so much of the cat in him, had Hamlet!'

'If they had half the sense of smell that we possess, everything would have been found out long ago,' said the parlour cat. 'To my mind, *The Merchant of Venice* was written entirely to prove that men are not aware of the value of cats. When Shylock says that some men cannot bear "a humble, necessary cat" any more than a harmless, necessary Jew, he says a thing that must go straight to the heart of every cat, from the first cat that caught fish in Egypt downwards.'

'I disagree with you there,' said the stage cat. 'I am inclined to think that our first ancestress, who is now drinking the cream of Paradise, came from Persia.'

'You may be right,' said the parlour cat, with a magnificent wave of her tail, and a velvet claw half unsheathed. 'We were talking about Shakespeare, I think. Did it ever occur to you that the "green-eyed monster" must have been a very big cat that was called jealousy? The word "green" proves it, without a doubt. Who ever saw a green-eyed dog or a green-eyed horse? "Monster" is very gratifying also. It is amazing to find what an idea men have of our size. Lord Roberts, for instance! He cannot sit in the room with me. He is a little man, of course. He has conquered a great many other men, of course; but he cannot conquer his aversion to cats. It must be because he thinks they are so big. He can't dislike green, as he comes from Ireland.'

'I thought we were talking about Shakespeare,' murmured the

stage cat suavely. Her eyes were not so good a green as those of the parlour cat.

The parlour cat stared at her for five minutes without blinking, and then pretended nothing had been said, and went on where she left off.

'A harmless, necessary cat!' she said. 'O my dear, how pathetic it is! *Il n'y a pas de chat nécessaire*. There is no such thing as a necessary cat, not even though Shakespeare thought there was! We can all be dispensed with, even the best rat-catcher amongst us. I buried a friend of mine the other day, a gentleman most eminent in his profession, and what do you think? They replaced him next day with a mouse trap!'

'Did they indeed?' said the stage cat, with deep sympathy. 'The play in *Hamlet*, the play that was written in very choice Italian, if you remember, was called *The Mouse Trap*. Shakespeare knew, what man better? that everything goes wrong in a family where they have mouse traps instead of cats. He was a cat himself, I feel quite sure of it.'

●

The climax of the farming year in the Yorkshire Dales is the Ram Sales. At Hawes in Wensleydale, the famous Swaledale shearing rams come under the auctioneer's hammer. They are a long-established part of the life of a hill farmer.

Alan Haydock went up to Yorkshire to make a programme about the sales for Radio 4 and one of the things he heard there was this poem, which is really a bit of a shaggy-ram story.

Binder String

Don't mind Bill Bates
That used to work for Drake at Badgers End,
There weren't a tool about the spot
That fellow couldn't mend.
From a hay fork to a harvester
Or any mortal thing,
Old Bill would always fix it
With a bit of binder string.

Ya day the Friesian bull got out
And rove and tore around,

127

No one durst go near him
As he roared and hooked the ground,
Till boss shouts, 'Bill, the bull's got out
And gone and broke his ring.'
So Bill lassoed the beggar
With a bit of binder string.

Bill courted Mabel seven years
And then said, 'Let's get wed.
I've got a table and some chairs
And granny's feather bed,
And there's half a ton of tatties
In yonder field that I can bring,
And I've made some handsome doormats
Out of thick, there binder string.'

So Mabel said, 'We'd best get wed
Afore they cut the hay.'
So they had a slap-up wedding
On the seventeenth of May,
But when he got to church Bill found
He'd forgot the ring,
So he had to marry Mabel
With a loop of binder string.

Next year a little daughter
Came to bless the happy pair,
With big blue eyes like saucers
And a tuft of ginger hair.
Now Bill he said to parson
At the baby's christening,
'See, her hair be just the colour
Of a bit of binder string.'

At last time came, poor old Bill died
And came to heaven's door;
He heard the angels singing there
And he was worried sore.
He said to good St Peter,
'I never learnt to sing,
I was always kept too busy
Mending things with binder string.'

'Don't worry,' good St Peter said,
'The good Lord understands.
He used to be a carpenter,
And likes to see folks use their hands.
We've plenty here who can sing,
Hast thou brought some binder string?'

And Bill do bide in heaven now,
He's very happy there,
He's got a little workshop
Round behind St Peter's chair.
And while the angels play their harps
And all the saints do sing,
Bill mends the little cherub toys
With bits of binder string.

●

While on the subject of animals, we ought to turn to those leading
exponents of animal songs, Michael Flanders and Donald Swann, who so
often have featured on *Pick of the Week*. In a programme on the BBC
World Service, Donald Swann, the surviving partner, insisted that they
were not animal-song writers. They were specialists in the mix between
animal and human. Johnny Morris called them 'animal anthropo-
morphics'. They used or invented animal fables to make observations
about humans. As an example, Donald Swann quoted Michael Flanders's
poem called 'Dead Ducks'.

The brontosaurus had a brain
No bigger than a crisp
The dodo had a stammer
The mammoth had a lisp
The auk was far too awkward
Now they're none of them alive
Each one, like man, had shown
Himself unfitted to survive.
This story points a moral
Now it's we who wear the pants
The extinction of these species
Holds a lesson for us ... Ants.

●

Have you ever wondered why a duck is called a duck, dead or otherwise? There seems no logical reason for it. Now, if it had been called a quack, you would understand it. That would have been an onomatopoeic name. There *are* certain birds who are called after the sound they make, and Denis Owen listed some of them in his Radio 4 programme *What's in a Name?* The obvious one is the cuckoo, but there are also the chiffchaff, the curlew and, best of all, Denis Owen thought, the hoopoe.

It certainly seems to say 'hoopoe', at least to my ear it does. This is a bird that's not very common in Britain; it occurs occasionally of course, but is much more widespread in the south, in Mediterranean countries. It certainly seems to say 'hoopoe' when you hear it in a rocky outcrop in Spain or Italy or southern France or somewhere. The generic name, that is to say the first of the two names for hoopoe, is *Upupa*, and that's Latin, it's a Latin word, it simply means 'hoopoe'. The second name, the species name, is *epops*, a very strange name *epops*, and that is Greek and also means 'hoopoe'; so the hoopoe is called *Upupa epops*.

But back to the chiffchaff – the Latin name of the chiffchaff is *Phylloscopus collybita*. The generic name comes from two Greek words which mean in effect a 'leaf watcher'; that is to say that the chiffchaff is a bird which takes an interest in what goes on in leaves, that's where it feeds. *Collybita*, the specific name, is also Greek, and it probably means moneychanger; the song is supposed to resemble the chink of coins being counted: chiff-chaff, chink-chink, chiff-chaff, chink-chink. It's interesting in this regard that one of the local French names for the chiffchaff is *compter d'argent*, which means 'money counter', and I can certainly with a bit of imagination imagine the sound of the chiffchaff indicating to at least some people the counting out of money.

●

It was Shakespeare who coined the phrase 'What's in a name?' which gave Denis Owen the title for his series – at least, that is what we are led to believe. Disputes about the authorship of the Shakespeare canon are not uncommon though, and the *Wizzalongawavelength* team added their thoughts on the matter in a song with words by Arthur Smith.

Troilus and Cressida, Midsummer Night's Dream,
The Merchant of Venice and Cymbeline,
Measure for Measure and Much Ado
About Nothing, The Tempest and Pericles too.

Timon of Athens, Macbeth and Othello,
Comedy of Errors, and All's Well That Ends Well-oh,
The Merry Wives of Windsor, Julius Caesar,
Edward II – no, that's another geezer,

Anthony and Cleopatra,
Romeo and Mrs Thatcher.

Mrs Thatcher is wrong and Juliet is right,
Like Coriolanus, King John and Twelfth Night,
Henry the Fourth, Fifth, Sixth and the Eighth
Should have been Henry the Seventh, but there ain't.

That's Henry the Fourth part one and part two,
Titus Andronicus, The Taming of the Shrew,
Richard the Second or Third, As You Like It,
Two Gents of Verona, and Hamlet, my favourite,
Love's Labour's Lost, Winter's Tale and King Lear,
These are the works of Francis Bacon.

●

One of the funniest playwrights of our own time, in my view, is Tom Stoppard. He is clearly a delight to work with, as his favourite producer, Peter Wood, testifies: 'I'm not interested in plays where the stage directions say, "Felicity walks slowly over to the french windows and picks up the photograph album and comes back to the mantelpiece." I mean, I much prefer the plays of Stoppard which begin with a lady stripping off on a trapeze or a pyramid of seventeen jumpers; immediately it gives me something to do. That's a very selfish view, but that's how I feel.'

Peter Wood was speaking on a BBC World Service profile of Tom Stoppard compiled and introduced by Dan Zerdin.

Stoppard's plays have been translated into twenty-one languages and they are regularly performed all over the world. His deliciously funny radio play *The Dog It Was That Died* won the Italia Prize. Amusing though they are, the plays do have an underlying seriousness and reveal a joy in words and literary jokes.

The critic Robert Cushman, who appeared on the World Service programme called *No Stopping Stoppard*, looked back to the playwright's first big success, *Rosencrantz and Guildenstern Are Dead*. It first appeared in 1967 and Cushman described it as 'pure *jeu d'esprit*'.

Rosencrantz and Guildenstern are rehearsing. They know they're going to have to come up against Hamlet and ask him exactly what he's got on his mind. They run through the scene they think they might have with him and, having asked him a few questions, Rosencrantz says, 'To sum up: your father, whom you love, dies, you are his heir, you come back to find that hardly was the corpse cold before his young brother popped on to his throne and into his sheets, thereby offending both legal and natural practice. Now why exactly are you behaving in this extraordinary manner?' That brings the house down always; but I think one reason it does bring the house down is, after all, the audience knows *Hamlet* and they know that the cause of Hamlet's madness is an endlessly discussed critical phenomenon – and suddenly here it all is put in absolutely basic terms, you wonder why anybody could ever have bothered about it. It's very funny, it's a literary joke; you don't get anything whatever out of the play if you don't know *Hamlet*.

●

Robert Cushman is drama critic of the *Observer*. A predecessor in the same line on the rival newspaper, the *Sunday Times*, was James Agate. He served as their drama critic from 1923 until 1947, and during that time he kept a daily journal which was published under the title *Selective Ego*. Using the journal as source material, Donald Bancroft compiled a programme for Radio 3 called *A Day in the Life of James Agate*.

Like that other great critic Neville Cardus, Agate had a passion for cricket and he recorded the following cricketing anecdote in his diary.

5 February 1943

Dined with Sir Pelham Warner at the Conservative Club. During dinner I contrived that the talk should be all about cricket. Among other things Plum Warner said that he once asked Ranji who in his opinion was the world's greatest batsman. Ranji replied, 'On a hard, fiery wicket, W. G., easily. But on all wickets, Charlo.' (This was Ranji's name for C. B. Fry.) Warner talked a lot about Fry. How he saw him make his record long jump, how the measurements were taken over and over again, and how the crowd shouted at the announcement of a world record. A lot more talk about the great cricketers of the past. In return for which I told him the story of how I bowled out W. G. Grace first ball. I was seven at the time, and the family was staying, I think, at either Blackpool or Llandudno. I was playing cricket on the sands, and presently a huge man with an immense black beard offered to bowl to me. He did not seem much good at bowling on the soft pitch with a tennis ball and I hit him all over the place. Being a well-brought-up little boy, I presently asked whether the gentleman would not like an innings, for which purpose I handed him my tiny bat. I bowled, the ball hit on a flat pebble and instead of bouncing slithered between the two walking-sticks which were the wickets, the Great Man having played about two foot over it! (He would have ricked his back if he had done anything else.) I remember my father, who was sitting on the promenade pretending to watch but actually reading the *Manchester Guardian*, laughing a great deal and telling me that I had bowled the world's greatest batsman. Which, let me confess, seemed a perfectly natural thing to do.

23 August 1944

The liberation of Paris was announced in the one o'clock news.

There is a transcendality of delirium about BBC matters which baffles me completely. I have known them fade out in the middle of the *Hallelujah Chorus*, the last page of *Tristan*, and the last ten bars on the *Hammerklavier Sonata*. And always in favour of popular muck. What I have never known them do is to fade out muck in any circumstances whatever.

Tonight I listened in to a special programme in honour of France. Incidentally, there was a long speech supposed to convey the views of the Man in the Street. This was uttered in an announcer's voice and contained the words 'garish' and 'pristine'. But let that pass.

The point is that tonight, of all nights, the BBC chose to fade out in the middle of the *Marseillaise*! After which a female voice said, 'You are now going to listen to *Cap and Bells*, a late-night revue with . . .' etc., etc. Gibbering like Othello, I rang up the BBC, and getting hold of the Biggest Noise in Charge, said, 'This is

James Agate speaking. Do you know that you have faded out in the middle of the *Marseillaise*. Goats and monkeys! May the Corporation rot, perish and be damned!' and rang off. Either the principle of elasticity is admitted by the BBC or it isn't. If it isn't, then it is surely a matter of timing and rehearsal. Why didn't they time and rehearse properly? If there are Other Factors I Know Nothing About, then the BBC must appoint a Director of Unknown Factors whose job it is to foresee and prevent gaffes like tonight's. Salary £5,000 a year.

Any gaffe to entail instant dismissal. Otherwise I expect to hear any evening now: 'At 11 a.m. today the General in Command of the Axis forces on the Rhine asked for an armistice, which the Allies granted on the following terms ...' *(Female voice interrupts.)* 'Listeners will now hear *Pop Goes the Weasel*, a late-night revue featuring Miss Naomi Thickhedde and the Uvula Boys ...'

When he went to Hollywood to make his name in pictures, David Niven was classified along with all the other 'extras'; his description was 'Anglo-

134

Saxon Type 2008'. The story of how he rose from that obscurity and became not only an international star but a bestselling author too is now legendary.

Sadly, David Niven died in 1983. Radio 2 presented a tribute to him which included the voice of Niven himself telling, in the way that only he could, a ribald and convoluted story about his early days in Hollywood when his desire to be a film star suffered a few setbacks.

I went to a Turkish bath, invited by Douglas Fairbanks's father, who I'd met in England when I was a little miserable officer in the regiment. I played golf with him. He found me on the street, in Hollywood Boulevard, wandering about, and he said, 'What are you doing wandering about?' And I said, 'I'm trying to be an actor.' And he said, 'Well, please don't ask me to help you because I simply can't. But come to the house any time you like – eat, drink, do anything you want to do, but don't ask me to try and help you. In the meantime why don't you come down to the studio and have a Turkish bath' – a steam, he called it. And really what I wanted was a nice hot lunch.

But he took me down to the steam and I sat on a marble slab between Darryl Zanuck and Joseph Schenck, who were then forming Twentieth Century Fox, Sid Grauman, who was the big man who owned all the theatres around the place, and Sam Goldwyn.

And I sat there thinking, this is my big chance. Here I am – not that I thought being naked would help much – but I sat there waiting for my big moment. And Fairbanks, who had a wild and idiotic sense of humour, knew I was absolutely broke then – I'd told him – and Fairbanks said, thinking he'd help me, 'Oh, Niven, what are you going to do this winter? Are you going to play polo or bringing the yacht round?' Well, I said, 'Polo, p-o-l-o, p-o-l-o,' and actually did faint.

I was carried out and put into a nice cold plunge, revived and came to to find Zanuck, who played polo and had his own team with a lot of international players in it, standing over me and saying to Fairbanks, 'Does he really play polo?' And Fairbanks, still thinking he could try to help, said, 'He played for the British army.' Which, of course, was absolute gibberish. I'd played twice, or something, in Malta on some ghastly animal. So the next thing Zanuck said to me, 'Well, come on over and play for me on Saturday.'

135

So I wind up at the polo club, the Riviera Country Club, on Saturday. When I arrived there, determined this will be my way into Twentieth Century Fox, he put me on this terrible horse called St George – that was a stallion that bit like a dog – and I had this hat, stick and whip which didn't fit, and tight trousers and also hundreds of people watching and huge internationals playing. And I had to mark Zanuck, and I thought this could be my big moment. I knew that I had to ride at him, ride at Zanuck, and stop him hitting the ball. So every time Zanuck got near the ball, I charged at him. He was Back in his team, I was Number One in ours, or something. And this awful animal, it wore a muzzle, it was muzzled this thing, St George, and one moment Zanuck was galloping with the ball and I came charging up from the back, and St George reached out and bit him in the arse. Good and right in the bum, through the muzzle. And Zanuck shrieking with pain. And now we'd galloped over the ball, which got trodden into the ground, and I saw this mushroom passing underneath us. And I took a vague swing at it with my stick, which passed underneath Zanuck's pony's tail, and the pony, being extremely goosey, clamped his tail to his behind and imprisoned the head of my stick. I'm tied onto the stick at one end with a leather thong, the other end is up the pony's bum, and Zanuck is shrieking at the other end, and this horrible triangle galloped past the stand. Now Fairbanks fell out of his chair he laughed so much. And I didn't work at Twentieth Century Fox for a long time.

●

Terry Wogan's meteoric rise from bank clerk to megastar is also legend. But in a Radio 4 profile of our hero the following heresy was pronounced by a fellow Irishman.

Eamonn Andrews: The fact is there is no such person as Terry Wogan. It's a syndicate of four people. The first is a former female impressionist from a fairground in County Donegal closed by the health authorities in 1959. The second is a man called Michael Paliaccio, an unfrocked priest from Pakistan, who gives elocution lessons in High Wycombe. And the third, known as Holy One, the illegitimate son of a golf professional from Killibegs, who exports left-hand clubs for right-hand players at The Garrick.

And the last is poor brother Stanislaus, a reformed alcoholic, son of a Kerry grass-importer who makes rosary beads for Protestant leprechauns. And may God forgive me for having made these disclosures.

●

In March 1984 at Westminster Abbey a plaque was unveiled to the memory of Sir Noel Coward. To commemorate the occasion, Glyn Dearman put together a programme for Radio 4 about a not-so-well-known aspect of Sir Noel's creative activity.

In parody of the literary pretensions of the twenties and thirties, Sir Noel anthologized in three volumes the work of a group of preposterously plausible poets and added his own suitably arcane commentary. For this tribute, Dearman dipped into one of these volumes.

Let us turn first to the work of Elihu Dunn. Born in Washington DC in 1896, he was described by Coward as 'A giant ... the music of his words crystallizes in the air like birdsong, he is the mouthpiece of his race calling them on to victory.'

> Ma skin is black
> As an ole black crow
> Ole black crow
> Vo dodeo do
> Ma pap was white
> As de wind blown snow
> Wind blown snow
> Vo dodeo do
> Ma Mammy was brown
> As chicken soup
> Chicken soup
> Boop oop a doop
> She knocked my Pappy
> For a loop
> For a loop
> Boop oop a doop
> Ma sis is pale
> As a piece of Gruyère
> Piece of Gruyère
> Halleluia
> But ma skin's black
> As an ole black crow
> Ole black crow
> Vo dodeo do.

Noel Coward: In writing an introductory preface to Jane Southerby Danks, it is odd to compare her early environment with that of her artistic contemporaries. Born in Melton Mowbray in 1897, she rode to hounds constantly, wet or fine, from the age of four onwards. Blauie's portrait *Musette on Roan* depicts her at the very beginning of her adolescence. From the first she shunned the company of the male sex, mixing only with her governesses. To one of whom, Madeleine Duphotte, she dedicated her first volume of poems, *Goose Grass*. The dedication is illuminating in its profound simplicity – 'To you, Madeleine, from me.'

Storm clouds in her relations with her mother began to gather on the horizon as early as 1912; indeed, in the May of this year we find her in Florence with Hedda Jennings, then at the height of her career.

In 1925 she published *Hands Down*, to be followed in the spring of 1926 by *Frustration*. In 1927 began her most prolific era, in St Tropez, where in company with Zale Bartlett and Thérèse Mauillac she wrote in French her celebrated 'Coucher de soleil pour violon' and 'Loup de mer'.

The poem included in this anthology is from her work of 1929–30 just after her quarrel with La Duchesse de la Saucigny Garonette (the 'Madame Practique' of 'Bon Jour') and expressing in its concrete outline her revulsion of feeling against the Sous-Realist School.

Announcer: 'Legend', by Jane Southerby Danks.

Jane Southerby Danks:
>Slap the cat and count the spinach
>Aunt Matilda's gone to Greenwich
>Rolling in a barrel blue
>Harnessed to a kangaroo
>Pock-marked Ulysses approaches
>Driving scores of paper coaches
>Eiderdowns and soda-water
>What a shame that Mrs Porter
>Lost her ticket for the play
>(Aunt Matilda's come to stay)
>Prod the melons, punch the grapes
>See that nobody escapes.

Tea is ready, ting-a-ling
Satan's bells are echoing
Father's like a laughing ox
Mimsying a paradox
Aunt Matilda's pet canary
Freda, Sheila, Bob and Mary
All combine to chase the bed
Now that Aunt Matilda's dead.

●

Victoria Jackson's poetry is all her own work. What it lacks in the writing she makes up for in the performance. When she appeared on *The Bob Monkhouse Show* on BBC2 she performed one of her numbers while doing a handstand and ended it by doing the splits. For the piece that follows, though, she adopted the relatively comfortable posture of lying on the floor. I think it was a move designed to get her nearer to her subject matter.

The Rug

The life of a rug is not sublime
You get walked on and stepped all over
   all of the time
You get beat when you're dirty
And when you're not clean
You get sucked by an incredibly
   painful machine.

My only joy is when a boy romances
   a girl by the fire
I get to hear their intimate whispers
   and feel their intense desire ...

●

In the Victorian age it was believed that such naughty goings-on were bad for your health, particularly if you were slightly poorly already. In those days, the disease of tuberculosis was not curable and so, in the absence of a suitable treatment, doctors used to send their wealthier patients to winter in what they felt were more health-giving climates.

In a Radio 3 talk, John Pemble, lecturer in history at Bristol University, outlined the debate that went on in medical circles of the day about which resorts were the best for the physical and, more importantly, the moral wellbeing of their patients. Promising results were achieved in Switzerland and Upper Egypt, but disappointments were experienced in the Mediterranean; resorts there were condemned for moral reasons.

It was a deeply rooted conviction in medical circles that dissipation and sensual indulgence were detrimental to health, and in the south the patient was tantalized by fatal allurements – warmth, natural beauty, art and fashionable society. 'Where climate supplies constant stimulation for the senses,' warned Dr James Johnson in 1830, 'passion will predominate over reason; and where the passions are indulged, the range of existence will be curtailed.' Consumption was often linked to loose living and reckless enjoyment, and the cosmopolitan brilliance and gaslit gaiety of Italy and the Riviera were anathema to Victorian doctors anxious to submit their patients to the healing influences of nature. Stories were current of the awful termination awaiting those who were tempted to turn their cures into carnivals. William Chambers, the retired Provost of Edinburgh, passed the winter of 1869–70 at Menton, and heard of 'a young gentleman of fortune with lungs much gone who, contrary to advice, attended a dancing party.' He collapsed, was carried out, and died in the passage. 'In that dance of death,' reflected Chambers mournfully, 'he had finished the last atom of lung, gaily ending his days in the revelry of a waltz.' Aghast, the ex-Provost observed the hectic vanity of invalids with one foot in the grave. 'Ladies bring enormous boxfuls of attire,' he reported, 'and wish to show it off somehow.' Only the previous season, the reigning beauty had been a young lady with one lung, 'which it was alleged she was doing all in her power to get rid of.' The Casino of Monte Carlo was condemned by medical men as a threat to healthy living. Dr Burney Yeo deplored what he called 'the dangerous seductions of the gaming tables', and Dr Edward Sparks complained that their noxious influence was infecting even Nice, Menton and San Remo, by attracting unwelcome visitors and enticing respectable families to ruin. And then there was the pernicious allurement of art. Nemesis lurked in galleries, museums and churches, in the form of sudden changes of temperature, fatigue, crowds, polluted air and chilly pavements.

●

There can have been few more heartbreaking moments in history than the second the news flashed across the world that President John F. Kennedy had been assassinated. Most of us who were alive on that dreadful day can remember exactly what we were doing when we heard the announcement. Rather fewer of us had the chance to meet Kennedy and experience first hand the extraordinary charisma he had.

Harold Macmillan, now Lord Stockton, as the British Prime Minister of the day, had many dealings with him. A Radio 4 documentary traced the *One Thousand Days* of John F. Kennedy, the brief period for which his presidency lasted. In the programme, Harold Macmillan conveyed the sense of loss most of us felt after the assassination; he recalled a time when the young President drove down to his home at Birchgrove in Sussex. Kennedy was at the height of his powers but had, as it turned out, only a few weeks to live.

He had a wonderful way of – a *royal* way of combining two things. Simplicity, and unbending, with dignity. And nobody could take a chance with him, or try it on. When he finally went off I can see him now walking out. We went out, said goodbye;

141

and we had arranged to meet either at the end of October or at the beginning of November to discuss the next plans, for the world. We felt sure we'd get this Test Ban Treaty, but after that, well, China, Russia. We'd have another meeting. I had still a bit of life in me, I perhaps could win the next election, he could win another, we might have five or six years together, to work on our plans. They were beginning to come off at last. Something was going to happen. And so he got in, and he sailed out over the valley. Lovely day, in June. And before the leaf had fallen, he'd gone. By a most brutal and terrible act.

●

It is difficult to reconcile ourselves to death, particularly the death of a loved one. Consolation is hard to find, but many *Pick of the Week* listeners drew a lot of comfort from some lines chosen by Lord Lichfield for *With Great Pleasure* on Radio 4. I have had more letters asking for copies of this than for anything else.

Patrick Lichfield himself had read the lines at the funeral of a close relative. They were written by the Reverend Canon Henry Scott Holland (1847–1918) and, though the context is sad, I hope that they will send you away happy at the end of the first *Pick of the Week* book.

Death is nothing at all ... I have only slipped away into the next room ... I am I and you are you ... whatever we were to each other that we are still. Call me by my old familiar name, speak to me in the easy way which you always used. Put no difference into your tone; wear no forced air of solemnity or sorrow. Laugh as we always laughed at the little jokes we enjoyed together. Play, smile, think of me, pray for me. Let my name be ever the household word that it always was. Let it be spoken without effect, without the ghost of a shadow on it. Life means all that it ever meant. It is the same as it ever was; there is absolutely unbroken continuity. What is this death but a negligible accident? Why should I be out of mind because I am out of sight? I am but waiting for you, for an interval, somewhere very near just around the corner ... All is well.

●

Acknowledgements

Thanks are due to the following for allowing us to reprint copyright material:

'Loch Ness Monster Song' by Edwin Morgan from *Poems of Thirty Years* (1982) reproduced by permission of Carcanet New Press; *International Language of Music* by Geoffrey Perkins reproduced by permission of the author; extract from *Faith, Hope and Clarity* reproduced by permission of John Dunn and Joan Paterson; extract from *Potted Tongues: Eccentric Languages* reproduced by permission of Richard Stilgoe and Will Green; definition of Christmas from *The Enlarged Devil's Dictionary* by Ambrose Bierce reproduced by permission of Victor Gollancz Ltd; two extracts from *What's in a Name* reproduced by permission of Dr Denis Owen; extracts from *Holy Bones* reproduced by permission of Libby Purves; extract from *Edmund Gosse* by Ann Thwaite reproduced by permission of Martin Secker and Warburg Ltd; 'A Nurses Reply' by Liz Hogben reproduced by permission of the author; extract from *Economics and the Public Purpose* by J. K. Galbraith reproduced by permission of Andre Deutsch; extract from interview with the Prime Minister from *Women of the World* reproduced by permission of the Rt Hon Margaret Thatcher, Natalie Wheen and Jenyth Worsely; extract from *Margaret Cavendish* reproduced by permission of Kathleen Jones; Women's Movement from *Alas Smith and Jones* by Jimmy Mulville with Mel Smith and Griff Rhys Jones, reproduced by permission of Jimmy Mulville; extract from interview with Christina Dodwell reproduced by permission of Christina Dodwell and Gavin Scott; extract from *The Other Half* reproduced by permission of Mrs Edwina Currie; *Yes, (Prime) Minister* reproduced by permission of the Rt Hon Margaret Thatcher; extract from *News Stand* by E. S. Turner reproduced by permission of *Punch*; extract from *Aristocrats* copyright © Robert Lacey reproduced by permission of Curtis Brown Ltd, London; 'Ode to a Tea Leaf' by Alexander Gleason reproduced by permission of the author; extract from *My Last Breath*,

the Alps reproduced by permission of John Pemble; extract from *One Thousand Days* reproduced by permission of the Rt Hon The Earl of Stockton OM.

AP8004017   00   05173   0148   00194